WORLD SERIES BASEBALL

WORLD SERIES
BASEBALL

THOMAS G. AYLESWORTH

HAMLYN

Published 1988 by
The Hamlyn Publishing Group Limited
A division of the Octopus Group Plc.
Michelin House, 81 Fulham Road,
London, SW3 6RB
and distributed for them by
Octopus Distribution Services Limited,
Rushden, Northamptonshire NN10 9RZ

Copyright © 1988 Bison Books Ltd

Produced by
Bison Books Ltd
176 Old Brompton Road
London SW5
England

ISBN 0 600 55765 0

Printed in Hong Kong

PAGE 2, ABOVE: Ross Grimsley of the Cincinnati Reds in the
1972 Series, in which Oakland Athletics won 4-3.

PAGE 2, BELOW: The Minnesota Twins celebrate their 1987
World Series victory.

CONTENTS

Introduction

A good case can be made that the World Series – the climax of baseball and, as such, a high point in America each year – was inevitable from the moment that baseball itself was born. Various occasions and individuals have been credited with its parentage, but as solid a claim as any for this 'blessed event' might be that day, 23 September 1845, when Alexander J Cartwright, a baseball-playing surveyor, proposed his set of rules to standardize the game. He had played for the New York Knickerbockers and other teams of amateur socialites in the area, and apparently had a mathematical mind. Among the rules that he established were the setting up of the official distances between bases and the rule that a runner would no longer be considered out if he were hit by a thrown ball.

These new rules were tested in a game the next year – 1846 – between the Knickerbockers and the New York Nine. The Knickerbockers were beaten badly, and had to pay off their side bets of a dinner per player. The game is also fondly remembered for what was perhaps the first rhubarb in the new age of baseball. The culprit was J W Davis, who swore at an umpire and was fined six cents.

Baseball boomed as an amateur sport under the Cartwright rules, and by 1858 there were more than 100 clubs in the northern states. Indeed, on 20 July 1858, the first admission charge was levied – 50 cents. The All-Star teams from Brooklyn and Manhattan played each other, and although they were amateurs, baseball was on its way toward becoming a commercial amusement. It was also on its way toward the annual showdown between the best that would eventually culminate in a World Series.

The first professional baseball team was founded in Cincinnati in 1869 by Harry Wright, an English-born professional cricket player, and the Cincinnati Red Stockings (later the Reds) were to change the face of baseball in America. Those Ohio-based play-for-pay athletes consistently beat the amateur clubs in the Midwest, and by 1871 the first professional league was founded – the National Association of Base-Ball Players [NABBP]. The league lasted for a mere five years.

In January of 1876 William Ambrose Hulbert, the owner of the Chicago club in the NABBP, held a meeting in Louisville, Kentucky, with the representatives of the Louisville, Cincinnati and St Louis clubs. He sold them his idea of a new league – the National League of Professional Base Ball Clubs. Teams in the eastern part of the United States soon joined the league, and the first game played was in Philadelphia on 22 April 1876, in which Boston defeated Philadelphia 6-5.

There were eight teams in the league – Chicago, Hartford, St Louis, Boston, Louisville, New York, Philadelphia and Cincinnati. Each team was to play 70 games, ten each against the other teams in the league, and Chicago won the first pennant – literally. The team's prize was a pennant that cost more than $100.

Over the years the Nationals had competition from other leagues, but most of them folded after a year or two. From 1894 to 1897 the first- and second-place teams in the league battled for a gaudy trophy called the Temple Cup.

It wasn't until 1899 that a strong rival league was formed, an occurrence that paved the way for the World Series as we know it today. That year, the Western League (a minor league) changed its name to the American League. In 1901 the league withdrew from the minor-league National Agreement and became a major league. The new league was made up of teams from Chicago, Cleveland, Milwaukee, Detroit, Baltimore, Philadelphia, Washington and Boston. The Chicago White Sox won the pennant that year.

Still, the National League was trying its best to ignore the upstarts. But the time of reckoning came in 1902 when the Americans actually outdrew the Nationals in attendance, by 2,200,000 to 1,683,000. Even more embarrassing was the fact that the American League teams outdrew the National League teams in the four cities to have teams in both leagues – Boston, Chicago, Philadelphia and St Louis (Milwaukee's team had been shifted to St Louis because it was the largest Midwestern city outside Chicago that didn't ban Sunday baseball).

Early in 1903 a National Commission was formed to oversee major-league baseball. The commission consisted of Harry C Pulliam and Ban Johnson, the presidents of the National and American Leagues, respectively; commissioner-at-large August Herrmann, the owner of the Cincinnati ball club; and a non-voting secretary. The way was clear for the first World Series.

ABOVE: A souvenir Temple Cup scorecard from the 1894 New York over Baltimore contest. This annual series was last played in 1897.

TOP AND MIDDLE RIGHT: A colorful scorecard for the 1929 Series, and program for the 1933 Series, capture the drama of America's national pastime.

RIGHT: A young vendor sells programs for the 1947 'Subway Series' between the Yankees and the Dodgers.

1903

Boston Somersets 5, Pittsburgh Pirates 3

The first World Series between the National and American Leagues was rather casually arranged. In August it was apparent that the Boston Somersets (later the Red Sox) of the American League and the Pittsburgh Pirates of the National League were going to win their league championships, and the presidents of the two clubs personally made plans to play the Series. At the end of the season, manager Jimmy Collins' Boston club finished 14 and a half games ahead of the Philadelphia Athletics and Fred Clarke's Pirates won by six and a half games over the New York Giants.

It was agreed that the winner of the Series would be the club that won the first five out of a possible nine games – the first three in Boston, the next four (if all were necessary) in Pittsburgh, and the other two, if necessary, in Boston. The Series was almost called off, however, because the Boston players' contracts ran only until 30 September. Since they felt that they would not be paid for playing in the Series, the Somerset players threatened to strike if they didn't get all the Boston gate receipts. Owner Henry J Killilea stopped the rebellion by offering the players extra money for playing – the players were to get $1182 and the owner $6999.56 for the Series. The Pittsburgh players did better, however, when owner Barney Dreyfuss tossed in his share, and each player received $1316.25, in addition to his salary.

On 1 October 1903 Pittsburgh won the first game of the first World Series ever played, 7-3, and after Boston won the second, 3-0, the Pirates won the next two, 4-2 and 5-4. So Boston was trailing, three games to one, after four contests. But in an amazing comeback the Somersets went on to sweep the final four games, 11-2, 6-3, 7-3 and 3-0.

Although Jimmy Sebring, the Pittsburgh right fielder, hit .367 for the Series and had the distinction of hitting the World Series' first home run in the first game (off none other than the legendary pitcher, Cy Young), the heroes of the 13-day Series were the pitchers. Deacon Phillippe of the Pirates pitched five complete games and was the winner in all three Pittsburgh victories. Boston pitchers were also intimidating. Bill Dinneen pitched four complete games, winning three of them, and Cy Young not only pitched three complete games, winning two of them, but also relieved early in the third game. The 1903 World Series netted approximately $50,000.

LEFT: Boston pitcher 'Big Bill' Dinneen pitched three wins and one loss in the 1903 Series, striking out 28 and turning in a 2.06 ERA performance.

ABOVE: The Pirates' owner Barney Dreyfuss contributed his share of Series money to his players.

OPPOSITE: Boston fans overflow the Old Huntington Avenue grounds to watch their team clinch the 1903 Series over the Pirates.

1904
No Series

There was no World Series played in 1904 because of some petty bickering on the part of the New York Giants against the American League. Giant owner John T Brush had had a long-standing feud with American League President Ban Johnson, and, added to that, Brush was irate that the American League had permitted a team to play in New York, which he considered his feifdom. When his Giants won the National League title in 1904, he refused to participate in post-season play.

He and his manager, the fiery John McGraw, issued a statement: 'There is nothing in the constitution or the playing rules of the National League which requires the victorious club to submit its championship honors to a contest with a victorious club in a minor league.' No requirement, yes. Minor league, no.

The big problem was probably that the American League pennant, at the time Brush made his decision, appeared to be going to the New York Highlanders (who had also been called 'The Porchclimbers' and 'The Burglars,' although Brush referred to them as 'The Invaders'), who were not to become the Yankees until 1913. The American League pennant went to the Boston Somersets, however, who took three games in their final series with New York to edge into first place at the end of the season. But Brush stuck by his guns.

Brush did recant, however, after the Boston club won the American League pennant. He announced that if his Giants won the 1905 National League pennant, they would play the American League champions. Brush even went so far as to establish some new rules for the World Series – rules that are still in effect. The nine-game format was scrapped for a best four-out-of-seven games, with mandatory participation in both leagues. Receipts for the first four games were to go to the players, with 10 percent to go to the National Commission and the rest to the managements of the competing clubs.

1905

New York Giants 4, Philadelphia Athletics 1

John T Brush's Giants did make it to the pennant in 1905, mostly on the strong right arm of the young pitcher, Christy Mathewson, who won 31 and lost but 9 that year. On the American League side, the pennant was won by the Philadelphia Athletics, and in their corner was their great southpaw pitcher, Rube Waddell, who had a 26-11 record. This Series was to be the first of three Series played between the Giants and the Athletics, the second of 10 Series the Giants would play under manager John McGraw, and the first of eight Series for Connie Mack, the Athletics' manager.

The eyes of the nation were to be on the confrontation between Mathewson and Waddell. Then, during the last two weeks of the season, Philadelphia was dealt what seemed like a mortal blow: the great Waddell injured his shoulder during some horseplay with his teammate, pitcher Andy Coakley, and Mack had no one to compete with Matty's magic.

The World Series was a pitcher's dream, since all five games ended in shutouts. Mathewson won the first game for the Giants, 3-0, on a four-hitter; the third game, 9-0, on another four-hitter; and the fifth game, 2-0, on a six-hitter. This was all done in a period of six days, and an amazing fact was that in the three games, Matty allowed only one walk while beating the Athletics,best starters (since Waddell was out) – Eddie Plank, Andy Coakley and Chief Bender. The only game won by Philadelphia was the second, which Bender won, 3-0, allowing but four hits.

It was certainly a Series of great pitching. In addition to the five shutouts, the Giants batted a puny .206 as a team, and the Athletics were even more miserable at the plate, hitting a terrible .161. There were no home runs in the Series, and the pitchers' earned run averages [ERA's] were phenomenal. Mathewson, McGinnity and Ames of the Giants, and Coakley of the Athletics all registered ERA's of 0.00, and Plank and Bender of the Athletics were not far behind with 1.06.

LEFT: The New York Giants' manager John 'Little Napoleon' McGraw (left) with his pitcher, Joseph McGinnity. The Giants' 4-1 championship win over the A's was aided by McGinnity's 0.00 ERA, a performance which included a game four shutout.

OPPOSITE TOP: A team photo of the 1905 New York Giants, World Series champions. Inset left is Christy Mathewson; inset right is shortstop Bill Dahlen.

OPPOSITE BOTTOM: The 1905 Philadelphia Athletics pose with their skipper, the young Connie Mack. The A's scored only three runs in the World Series that year, all of them in game two.

Champions of 1905—McGraw's Giants. On the Club Roster Were Such Names as Bresnahan, Wiltse, "Dummy" Taylor, George Brown, Devlin, McCormick, McGinnity, McGann, Ames, Bowerman, Gilbert and Marshall

NEW YORK GIANTS
~1905~

1906

Chicago White Sox 4, Chicago Cubs 2

This was the year of the first World Series between two clubs that played in the same city – the Chicago Cubs and the Chicago White Sox. And it was one of the greatest upsets in the history of post-season play. Manager Frank Chance's Cubs had won the pennant in the National League, setting a season record of 116 wins, finishing 20 games ahead of the New York Giants. On the other hand, the White Sox, called 'The Hitless Wonders,' won the American League pennant from the New York Highlanders by three games with a pathetic team batting average of .228 – the lowest in the American League. The only reason they won the pennant was an amazing 19-game winning streak in August.

The Cubs also had the services of the great pitcher, Mordecai 'Three Finger' Brown, who had a 26-6 record that year with an overwhelming 1.04 earned run average. The other star pitchers for the Cubs were Jack Pfeister (20-8), Ed Reulbach (19-4) and Carl Lundgren (17-6), and the team pitching as a whole had an ERA of 1.76. The Cubs also led the league in hitting, and there was no way that the Sox could win the Series – on paper, that is.

But White Sox manager Fielder Jones also had a fine pitching staff. There were Big Ed Walsh and Frank Owens, both righthanders, and southpaws Nick Altrock and Georgetown Doc White.

The Series was another pitcher's dream. Reulbach pitched a one-hitter in the second game, and in the third and fourth games Walsh and Brown, respectively, pitched two-hitters. So overpowering was the pitching that the Cubs batted .196 as a team and the White Sox .198.

Altrock beat Brown in the opener, 2-1, with each team getting but four hits. In the second game, the Cubs evened the Series when Reulbach won his one-hitter, 7-1. The Sox took the lead in the third game – Walsh's two-hitter – by a score of 3-0, and the Cubs evened it up in the fourth with Brown's two-hitter, by a score of 1-0. Then the White Sox put it away, winning the final two games, 8-6 and 8-3. The miracle had occurred.

ABOVE: White Sox southpaw Guy Harris 'Doc' White pitched an 8-3 win over the Cubs in the Series' deciding game.

LEFT: The Cubs' ace, Mordecai 'Three Finger' Brown, won one but dropped two games in the Series.

OPPOSITE: White Sox pitcher Big Ed Walsh warms up. During the 1906 regular season Walsh won 17 games, 10 of them shutouts. With a 1.80 Series ERA and 17 strikeouts in 15 innings, Walsh hurled the Sox to two Series wins.

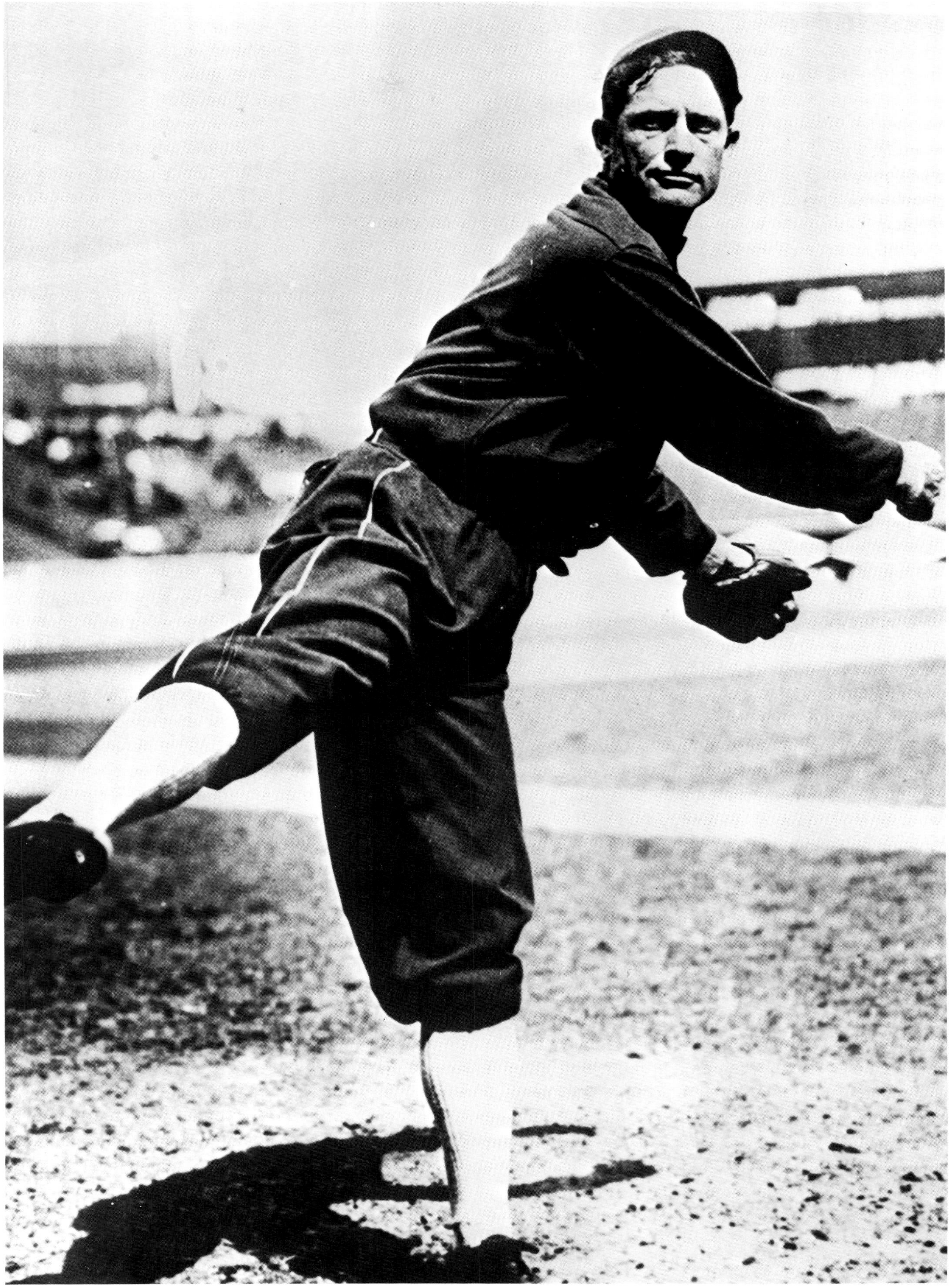

1907

Chicago Cubs 4, Detroit Tigers 0, 1 tie

The year after their surprising defeat in the World Series, the Chicago Cubs under manager Frank Chance were back at the top, and with a vengeance. This time they had outdistanced the second-place Pittsburgh Pirates by 17 and a half games. Aided by an outstanding infield that featured the legendary double play combination of Joe Tinker to John Evers to Frank Chance, and continued excellent pitching by Mordecai 'Three Finger' Brown, Orval Overall and Ed Ruelbach, Chicago recorded an overall team earned run average of 1.73, the lowest in National League history.

Their opponents in the World Series were Hugh Jenning's Detroit Tigers, a team that featured one of the greatest players ever to play the game – the right fielder Ty Cobb, who hit .350 that year to win the first of his nine batting titles. Strong pitching from Wild Bill Donovan, George Mullin, Ed Killian and Ed Siever had helped the Tigers edge out the Philadelphia Athletics by one and a half games for the pennant.

This time the Cubs were not to be denied. After the first game ended in a 3-3 tie, being called on account of darkness, Chicago went on to sweep the Tigers, four games to none, making Detroit the first team in history to be shut out in the World Series. The first game was rather an oddity. Bill Donovan, the star pitcher for the Tigers, had a particular piece of misfortune when catcher Charlie Schmidt failed to hold a third strike in the ninth inning, which cost the righthanded pitcher a 3-2 victory. The pitch would have retired the side, but the error let the tying run score from third. The play generated some suspicion because the Tiger player representative, Herman 'Germany' Schaefer, had asked the Baseball Commission in a pre-series meeting what its policy would be on sharing gate receipts if one of the first four games ended in a tie. The commission deliberated and ruled that in the event of a tie, the players would have a share in the first five games, rather than the first four. So many cynics wondered if the game had been rigged. In an investigation, no skullduggery was found.

At any rate, the Cubs won the second game, 3-1, behind Pfiester, the third, 5-1, behind Ruelbach, the fourth, 6-1, behind Overall, and the final game, 2-0, behind Brown. They certainly deserved to win, out-hitting the Tigers .257 to .208, stealing 18 bases, and featuring Harry Steinfeldt, the third baseman, hitting .471, and Johnny Evers, the second baseman, hitting .350.

LEFT: Tiger pitcher George Mullin warms up. After turning in his third straight 20-win season, Mullin dropped two games in the Series.

ABOVE: Cub first baseman manager Frank Chance, who scored three runs on three hits in the 1907 Series.

Tiger manager Hughie Jennings gestures on the sidelines. In the first three of his 14 years as Detroit manager, Jennings won the pennant.

1908

Chicago Cubs 4, Detroit Tigers 1

The Cubs and the Tigers were at it again in 1908. Chicago, in taking their third straight flag, had had a fierce battle with the New York Giants and Pittsburgh. On 23 September 1908, the Cubs played the Giants at the Polo Grounds in a game which could have decided the pennant. In the bottom on the ninth the score was tied 1-1 and the Giants had men on first and third. Then came Fred Merkle's 'bonehead' play. Giant shortstop Al Bridwell hit a single to center, and the man on third scored what should have been the winning run. The 19-year-old Merkle was on first base, and rather than run to touch second base, turned and ran to the clubhouse, thinking the game was over. However, Cub second baseman Johnny Evers got the ball (or at any rate *a* ball) and touched second base, turning the hit into a forceout at second. The game was called on account of darkness and it was registered as a tie. The Cubs and Giants ended the season in a tie, a playoff game was scheduled, and Chicago's Mordecai 'Three Finger' Brown beat Christy Mathewson, 4-2, for the pennant.

The American League race was also a cliffhanger. The Tigers won the pennant with the Cleveland Indians a half game back at season's end and the White Sox one and a half games out.

History repeated itself in the World Series, with the Cubs bowling over the Tigers. The Cubs leaped off to a 10-6 win in the first game, with Mordecai 'Three Finger' Brown the winner, then in the second game, Overall pitched them to a 6-1 triumph. Detroit came back in the third, winning 8-3, with George Mullin striking out eight Cubs. It was all downhill from then on, with Chicago winning 3-0 (Brown pitching) in the fourth game and 2-0 (Overall on the mound) in the fifth.

Even with a .368 batting average, Ty Cobb had not been able to do it all. He got seven hits and stole two bases, but the Tigers had won only one game and had been shut out in the last two. The people of Detroit

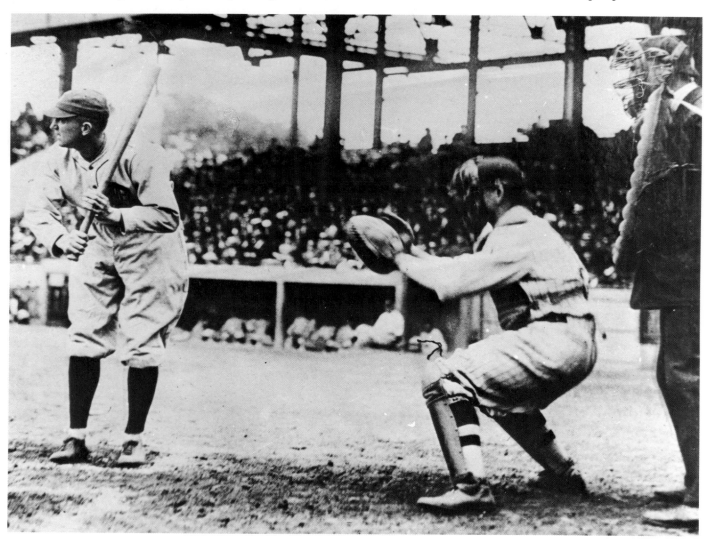

ABOVE: The Giants' Fred Merkle, whose baserunning blunder marred an otherwise fine career.

RIGHT: After the 'Merkle' play, umpire Hank O'Day called the Giants-Cubs game a tie, necessitating the playoff that the Cubs won.

LEFT: Detroit's brilliant Ty Cobb at bat.

seemed to sense the impending devastation. The last game was played in Detroit, and only 6201 people showed up to see the carnage at Bennett Field – a World Series record for lack of enthusiasm.

1909

Pittsburgh Pirates 4, Detroit Tigers 3

In 1909 the World Series, for the first time in history, went to the full seven games before the Pittsburgh Pirates beat the Detroit Tigers, four games to three. Pittsburgh had won 110 games that year, finishing six and a half games ahead of the Cubs, and the Tigers had taken the American League pennant by three and a half games over the Athletics.

The Pirates' big weapon was John Peter 'Honus' Wagner, possibly the greatest shortstop in baseball history, who had batted .339 during the season. And the great Ty Cobb was the star right fielder for the Tigers. Cobb had hit .377 that season. In the Series Wagner outhit Cobb by .333 to .231. But the star of the Series was a rookie Pirate pitcher, Charles 'Babe' Adams. He had a 12-3 record for the season, and had been eclipsed by the Pirate pitchers Howard Camnitz, Vic Willis, and lefthander Al Leifield, who had won 25, 22 and 19 games, respectively. But in the Series, the big three did not win a game, while the youthful Adams won three of Pittsburgh's triumphs – the fourth going to Nick Maddox, who had won 13 games during the season.

Pittsburgh won the first game, 4-1, with Adams beating Detroit pitcher George Mullin on a six-hitter, but the Tigers came right back to win the second game, 7-2, with Bill Donovan beating Camnitz on a five-hitter. Then it was the Pirates' turn in the third game, and Maddox threw a ten-hitter to beat Oren Summers, 8-6. Once again Detroit fought back in the fourth game, which Mullin won over Leifield, 5-0. Continuing the on again-off again Series, Pittsburgh won the fifth game, 8-4, behind Adams (Summers was the loser). Again Detroit stormed back, winning the sixth game, 5-4 – Mullin again the winner, beating Willis on a seven-hitter. The final game was rather an anticlimax, with Pittsburgh jumping on Tiger pitcher Bill Donovan for two runs in the second inning, never to be headed. Adams won his third game in the Series, 8-0, by throwing a six-hitter. The public was beginning to wonder just how major the American League was, since it had won but a single World Series in nine years. But times were about to change.

LEFT: Hall of Famer Ty Cobb at bat. In 1909, the fifth year of his illustrious 24-year career, Cobb led the league in hits (216), runs (116), RBI's (107), stolen bases (76), and batting average (.377). In the Series that year, Cobb was out hit by the Pirates' great shortstop, Honus Wagner.

RIGHT: The Pirates' slugger, Honus Wagner, slaps an infield hit. Wagner batted .333 in the 1909 Series, with four runs and six RBI's, helping his team win it all.

1910

Philadelphia Athletics 4, Chicago Cubs 1

The Cubs returned to the winner's circle again in 1910, winning their fourth National League championship in five years by a 13-game margin over the second-place Giants. Chicago fielded essentially the same team that had been successful as far back as 1906 – a team that featured the fine double play combination of Joe Tinker (shortstop), Johnny Evers (second base) and Frank Chance (first base). It was of this trio that Franklin P Adams had written in his newspaper column in July of 1910 – perhaps the second most famous poem about baseball ever penned (counting 'Casey at the Bat' as number one):

These are the saddest of possible words
Tinker to Evers to Chance.
Trio of Bear Cubs and fleeter than birds
Tinker to Evers to Chance.

Thoughtlessly pricking our gonfalon bubble,
Making a Giant hit into a double,
Words that are weighty with nothing but trouble
Tinker to Evers to Chance.

The Philadelphia Athletics ran away from the rest of the American League in 1910, finishing 14 and a half games ahead of the second-place New York team, and they were expected to be no match for the more experienced Cubs. But these youthful players under the guidance of Connie Mack surprised the country by a 4-1 Series margin, and Mack later said that he should have taken the Series in a sweep, but he let sentiment get in the way of his better judgment in the fourth game. With his club ahead 3-2 in the eighth inning, Mack

LEFT: Cubs second baseman Johnny Evers (left) and shortstop Joe Tinker, of the famous double play combination – Tinker to Evers to (Frank) Chance. Tinker batted .333 in the 1910 Series. Both Tinker and Evers were elected to the Hall of Fame in 1946.

OPPOSITE: Philadelphia's Eddie Collins, pictured at a later time in a White Sox uniform (which he wore 12 years), began and ended his 25-year career with the A's. Collins was red-hot for the 1910 Series, his .479 average helping his team win it all.

dismissed a hunch to have Topsy Hartsel pinch-hit for Ira Thomas, and Thomas ruined a rally by hitting into a double play with the bases full. The Cubs went on to score a run in the ninth and another in the tenth to win, 4-3.

But the rest of the Series was strictly a Philadelphia clinic. The Athletics won the first game, 4-1, with Chief Bender beating Orval Overall, and the second game, 9-4, with Jack Coombs beating Mordecai 'Three Finger' Brown. The third game went to the Athletics, 12-5 – Coombs again, this time beating Harry McIntire. Brown was the winner and Bender the loser in the fourth game, and Philadel-

phia ended the Series with a 7-2 triumph, with Coombs winning his third game, defeating Brown.

It was really Philadelphia all the way. The Athletics slammed the Cubs with a team batting average in the Series of .316, a record that was to stand until 1960. The Cubs hit a meager .222. The Athletics scored 35 runs in five games – an average of seven a game. Eddie Collins, the second baseman for Philadelphia, hit .429 and stole four bases, and third baseman Frank Baker hit .409. Even pitcher Jack Coombs batted .385. And with Johnny Evers on the bench with a broken leg, the Cubs didn't have a chance.

1911

Philadelphia Athletics 4, New York Giants 2

The Philadelphia Athletics under Connie Mack returned to the World Series once more in 1911. Although the Mackmen didn't move into first place for the pennant until late in the season, they went on a tear, ending up ahead of the second-place Tigers by 13 and a half games. The Giants were the representatives of the National League after almost literally pilfering the pennant, having stolen an amazing 347 bases during the season. The matchup between these two teams resulted in one of the most hotly contested of all Series.

The Series that year didn't get underway until 14 October because the National League schedule ran until 12 October – Columbus Day. And since rain held up play for six days between the third and fourth games, the Series was not over until 26 October.

The first game was played at the Polo Grounds in New York before 38,281 fans – the largest World Series crowd up to that time. The game was a brilliant pitching duel between the Giants' ace, Christy Mathewson, and the Athletics' star hurler, Chief Bender. New York won the game, 2-1. In the second game it was Eddie Plank for Philadelphia against Rube Marquard, and the Athletics won, 3-1, on Frank Baker's sixth-inning two-run homer. The third game pitted Mathewson against Jack Coombs, and Baker was again the hero, hitting another homer to tie the score in the ninth inning. Philadelphia won in the eleventh, 3-2, when the Giants committed two fateful errors, permitting two runs to score.

Then the rains came. After nearly a week of precipitation, Mathewson and Bender were well rested. The Athletics won the fourth game, 4-2. The Mackmen seemed to have the fifth game in the bag, going into the ninth inning with a 3-1 lead. But Coombs had pulled a muscle in his side in the sixth inning, and had to be replaced by Eddie Plank in the tenth, after the Giants had tied the score in the ninth. New York pitcher Otis

OPPOSITE: A's third baseman Frank 'Home Run' Baker earned his nickname in the 1911 Series, when he hit two crucial homers.

LEFT: Philadelphia's Eddie Plank pitched a 23-8 season in 1911; in the Series he pitched a complete game win, but lost game five in relief.

BELOW: The Giants' ace Rube Marquard led the league in winning percentage, with .774, and in strikeouts, with 237, in 1911. The Hall of Fame pitcher did not fare as well in the Series that year, however, as he was shelled by Baker for a loss in game two.

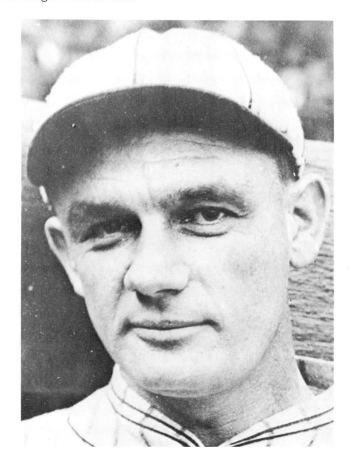

'Doc' Crandall had driven in a run himself with a double. Then the Giants scored a run in the bottom of the tenth off Plank and won the contest, 4-3. But the Athletics crushed the Giants in the sixth and final game to take the Series four games to two. Philadelphia won the game, 13-2, beating Leon Ames (the eventual loser), George Wiltse and Rube Marquard, as Bender won his fourth World Series game and second of the Series. In the Series, the Giants had been outhit .244 to .175.

It was in this Series that Frank Baker earned his nickname, 'Home Run' Baker. His two home runs in two days convinced New York's catcher Chief Meyers that the American League team must have some mysterious access to the Giants' signals. While Baker's lifetime record of 100 home runs does not seem spectacular by today's standards, the game then was being played with a 'dead' ball.

1912

Boston Red Sox 4, New York Giants 3, 1 tie

In 1912 American League batters were overwhelmed by the Boston pitcher Smokey Joe Wood, who was but 22 years old. Fenway Park had opened that year and Wood posted a 34-5 season to mark the occasion. He struck out 258 batters, pitched ten shutouts and batted .290 to boot. The Red Sox set an American League record that year with 105 victories, and topped the second-place Washington club by 14 games. The New York Giants repeated handily in the National League, winning 103 games and ending ahead of the second-place Pirates by 10 games. They had gotten a jump on the league when Rube Marquard had run up a streak of 19 wins early in the season.

The World Series of 1912 has been characterized as sloppy but excitingly close, with the Sox beating the Giants four games to three, with one tie. Wood defeated Jeff Tesreau in the Polo Grounds opener, 4-3. Then came the exciting 6-6 tie in Boston the next day. At the end of nine innings, the score was tied, 5-5. Both teams scored one run in the tenth, and the game was called on account of darkness at the end of the eleventh.

Rube Marquard of the Giants then put New York back in the Series with a 2-1 decision over Bucky O'Brien, but Boston gained a big three-to-one edge by winning the next two games, Wood defeating Tesreau again, 3-1, and Hugh Bedient winning a brilliant 2-1 decision over Christy Mathewson.

The Giants may have been down 3-1, but they weren't out. They knocked out Tom O'Brien and Joe Wood in the first innings of games six and seven and tied up the Series with impressive 5-2 and 11-4 victories.

With the Series tied at three games each, the final game was a cliffhanger. Mathewson was opposed by Bedient. The Giants scored in the third inning, but pinch-hitter Olaf Hendriksen, batting for Bedient, hit a double with a man on base, tying the score in the seventh. Harry Hooper had already saved the Series for Boston with a dazzling catch to rob Larry Doyle of a homer in the fifth inning. Wood replaced Bedient on the mound and the score stood at 1-1 going into the tenth. The Giants scored a run in the top of the tenth, but when the Red Sox came to bat in the bottom of the inning, the Giants' center fielder, Fred Snodgrass, committed the celebrated error, soon known as 'Snodgrass' $30,000 muff,' by dropping an easy fly ball hit by pinch-hitter Clyde Engle. After Harry Hooper was retired, Steve Yerkes walked. Tris Speaker singled in Engle with the tying run and sent Yerkes to third. Yerkes scored the winning run on Larry Gardner's long outfield fly to Josh Devore, bringing an exciting end to the hard-fought contest.

OPPOSITE TOP: Managers Jake Stahl and John McGraw confer with the umpires in the opening game of the 1912 World Series.

RIGHT: The New York Giants pose on the field at the Polo Grounds before a 1912 World Series game. The car was presented to Chalmers Award winner Giant Larry Doyle, National League MVP.

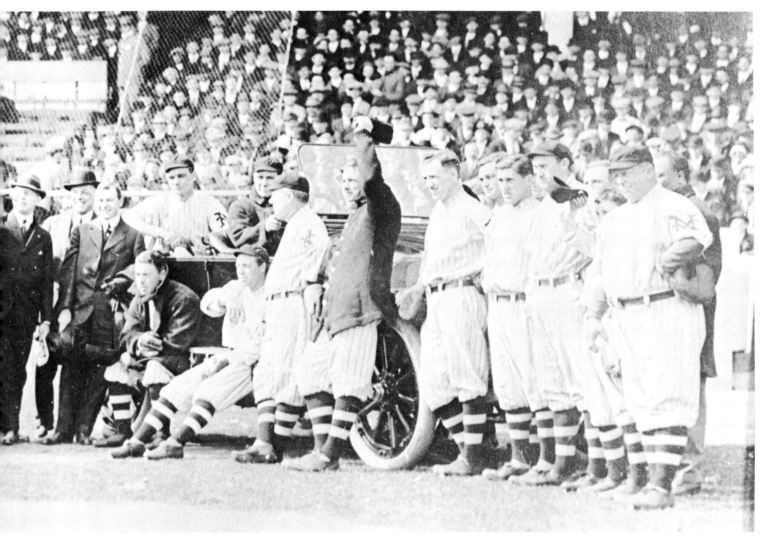

1913

Philadelphia Athletics 4, New York Giants 1

The Philadelphia Athletics were back in the Series in 1913, as were the New York Giants. This was the third time within a period of nine years that they had faced each other in the fall classic. The Athletics had finished six and a half games ahead of the Washington Senators, and had won a mere 96 games during the regular season. The Giants had won 101, and were considered to have an excellent chance against Connie Mack's team. Then John McGraw's aggregation suffered a series of disasters. Center fielder Fred Snodgrass suffered from a charley horse and could make only two brief appearances in the Series. First baseman Fred Merkle also suffered a leg injury, and while he missed but one game, he was limping throughout the Series. The first-string catcher, Chief Meyers, suffered a broken finger in the first game.

The Philadelphia legend, pitcher Chief Bender, won the opener, beating Rube Marquard 6-4 by scattering 11 hits. The second game was New York's only highlight when they won the game, 3-0. Eddie Plank had blanked the Giants for nine innings, but in the tenth, the Giants, behind the pitching of Christy Mathewson, stormed back with three runs, and that was it.

The third game was a disaster for the Giants. Connie Mack's men scored three runs in the first inning and two in the second, and the contest was never in doubt. Joe Bush, a 21-year-old pitcher, beat Jeff Tesreau, 8-2. It was Chief Bender in the fourth game again, and he beat Al Demaree, 6-5 – his sixth World Series win.

In the final game, Mathewson, who had pitched in 11 World Series games and won five, went down to defeat, 3-1. Eddie Plank, the Philadelphia pitcher, had finally vanquished his old rival. That was it – Philadelphia four wins, New York one win.

The Athletics had batted .264 against the Giants' .201. Mack had gone through the whole Series using but 12 players, playing only two catchers and three pitchers.

LEFT: The Giants' third baseman, Buck Herzog, tries to beat out an infield grounder in game two of the 1913 Series. Herzog went 1 for 19 in the Series.

ABOVE: A's Frank Baker is out at third base in the fourth inning of the Series' first game. Baker's three RBI's and three hits, including a two-run homer, helped his team to a 6-4 win.

1914

Boston Braves 4, Philadelphia Athletics 0

The 1914 season gave baseball fans one of the most exciting pennant races and World Series of all time – featuring the 'Miracle Braves' from Boston. On 19 July the Braves were in last place, but after an incredible winning streak they climbed to second place by 10 August, six and a half games behind John McGraw's Giants. They moved into first place on 2 September, slipped briefly to third, and returned to first on 8 September. After winning 60 of their last 76 games, they took the National League pennant by 10 and a half games over the Giants, the first time a club other than the Giants, Cubs or Pirates had taken the pennant since 1900.

The manager of the Braves, George Stallings, had said early in the season that 'I have 16 pitchers, all of them rotten,' but Dick Rudolph (27-10), Bill James (26-7) and George Tyler (16-14) did the job anyway. In the center of the infield were superstars Walter 'Rabbit' Maranville (shortstop) and Johnny Evers (second base).

Still, Connie Mack's Athletics were expected to take care of the Braves with ease in that year's World Series. With their '$100,000 infield,' the Philadelphia team had won the American League pennant by finishing eight and a half games ahead of the Red Sox. And to make the Athletics even stronger favorites, Red Smith, the Braves' regular third baseman, broke his leg just before the Series began. But the Athletics were destined to be the first team in the history of the World Series to be beaten in four straight games.

Rudolph was the winning pitcher in the first game, in which he beat Chief Bender, 7-1 – a game in which Philadelphia was never ahead. James won the second game, 1-0, beating Eddie Plank with a two-hitter. James came back in the third game to relieve starter George Tyler after 10 innings, beating Joe Bush, 5-4. The *coup de grace* was delivered by Rudolph again, when he defeated Bob Shawkey, 3-1.

The hero of the Series was undoubtedly Hank Gowdy, the Boston catcher. He had hit a mediocre .243 during the season, but came into his own in the Series – batting .545. His six hits included one single, three doubles, a triple and a home run, and he was the first player ever to hit over .500 in a World Series. He also walked five times.

Philadelphia hit a pathetic .172 as a team, against Boston's .244. Connie Mack then sold off the team's best players and the Athletics were headed for last place in the American League.

BELOW: Philadelphia's Amos Strunk is out at the plate in the second inning of the Series' first game. The A's scored one run to Boston's seven.

RIGHT: The Miracle Braves' third baseman Charlie Deal makes a throw in the Series' first game, at Shibe Park. Deal moved to St Louis the following year, and finished his career with the Cubs.

1915

Boston Red Sox 4, Philadelphia Phillies 1

Another Philadelphia team made it to the World Series in 1915. It was the Phillies, who had won the National League pennant with a .592 won-lost percentage, the lowest to capture a flag up to that time. The magic ingredient that took manager Pat Moran's men to the top that year was the legendary pitcher Grover Cleveland Alexander, the righthander who won 31 games – 12 of them shutouts. There was also Gavvy Cravath, the right fielder who hit 24 home runs that year to break Wildfire Schulte's record of 21. This remained the record until Babe Ruth started rewriting the home run books. In the American League the Boston Red Sox had edged out the Detroit Tigers by two and a half games.

After Alexander – Alex the Great – had defeated Ernie Shore in the first game of the Series, the Phillies fell apart. The first game ended at 3-1 as Alexander scattered eight hits to the Phillies' five. A guest at the second game was President Woodrow Wilson, who had come all the way from Washington to Philadelphia to throw out the first ball, which was returned to him by umpire Charlie Rigler for a souvenir. The game was close, but Boston defeated Philadelphia, 2-1, on George Foster's three-hitter that beat Erskine Mayer.

Things continued to go Boston's way in the third game, which was another 2-1 squeaker. Hubert 'Dutch' Leonard threw a three-hitter to beat Alexander as the winning run scored in the bottom of the ninth inning. The fourth game was yet another 2-1 thriller, the Sox winning as Ernie Shore, who had lost the first game to the Phillies, came back to beat George Chalmers. The final game was another close one. The Red Sox had to score two runs in the eighth and one in the ninth to win, 5-4, behind Foster, who beat Eppa Rixey. On the bench, eating his heart out, was Babe Ruth, the young southpaw hurler of the Boston club, who had been the pitcher with the best winning percentage in the American League that year, with 18 wins and six losses. Manager Bill Carrigan used the Bambino only once in the Series – as a pinch hitter.

LEFT: Boston's Larry Gardner is forced out by Philly second baseman Bert Niehoff in the Series' fifth and final game. Boston won the game, 5-4, and the Series, four games to one.

ABOVE: The Phillies' catcher Ed Burns scores their only run in the third inning of the Series' third game.

RIGHT: Philadelphia's Gavvy Cravath and Boston's Tris Speaker shake hands before a 1915 Series game. Cravath's hit in game four bounced over Speaker's head for a triple, denying Sox pitcher Ernie Shore his shutout as Cravath was then singled in for the Phillies' only run.

One of the heroes of the Series was George 'Rube' Foster, who not only pitched the Red Sox to two victories, but also went four for eight at the plate for a .500 batting average. Boston outfielders Duffy Lewis and Harry Hooper hit .444 and .350 respectively, and Hooper hit two homers in the last game. As a team, the Sox outhit the Phillies .264 to .182. The Phillies were not to return as National League champions until 1950.

1916

Boston Red Sox 4, Brooklyn Dodgers 1

Brooklyn took the National League pennant in 1916, becoming the third National League team in a row to appear in its first Series. The Brooklyn team then was called the Robins, after portly manager Wilbert Robinson. 'Uncle Robbie' drew fans to Ebbets Field with his clownish antics, but it was his skill in developing pitchers that won him the pennant. Brooklyn finished two and a half games in front of the Phillies at the end of a season-long dogfight among Brooklyn, Philadelphia and the Boston Braves.

The American League pennant was won by the Red Sox again, even though they had traded away their star center fielder, Tris Speaker, to Cleveland. Babe Ruth brought his 23-game winning record to the Series.

'Uncle Robbie' had planned to beat the Sox largely with southpaws, especially Rube Marquard and Sherry Smith. Marquard was the starting pitcher in the first game, and he faced Ernie Shore. Boston was the winner, 6-5, but Brooklyn almost pulled out a win by scoring four runs in the top of the ninth. It was Boston again in the second game, 2-1. Making his first start in a World Series, left-handed pitcher Ruth beat Sherry Smith in the longest game played in Series history. The Babe pitched scoreless ball after Chief Meyers, the Brooklyn center fielder, hit a home run in the first inning. The game went 14 innings and Ruth gave up but six hits.

Brooklyn's lone victory came in the third game, when Jack Coombs defeated Carl Mays, 4-3. The fourth game saw Dutch Leonard throw a five-hitter at Brooklyn to come up with a 6-2 victory over Marquard. The fifth game marked Shore's second victory in the Series, as he outpitched Jeff Pfeffer with a three-hitter and the Red Sox won, 4-1. The game was never in doubt after the Sox went ahead 3-1 in the bottom of the third inning. At the end it was Boston, four games to one.

Red Sox Tilly Walker slides safely into third base for a long triple in the first inning of the 1916 Series' first game. Boston went on to take the game from Brooklyn, 6-5.

ABOVE: Wilbert 'Uncle Robbie' Robinson, pictured in uniform. Robinson played catcher for 17 years, managing Baltimore his last year (1902), then managed the Brooklyn club from 1914 to 1931. He was elected to the Hall of Fame in 1945.

If Brooklyn had a hero, it was probably Casey Stengel, the right fielder, who hit .364 for the Robins. On the Boston side, once again Duffy Lewis and Harry Hooper gave opposing pitchers headaches with averages of .353 and .333, respectively. Jack Coombs had run his World Series record to five victories and no defeats.

ABOVE: Red Sox pitcher Dutch Leonard warms up before the start of the Series' game four. Leonard pitched a complete game, allowing no runs and only three hits after the Dodgers' two-run first inning.

1917

Chicago White Sox 4, New York Giants 2

The Chicago White Sox stopped the Red Sox' string of pennants in 1917. The Chicago club had pitching that was on a par with Boston's, a strong infield, and the peerless Shoeless Joe Jackson in left field.

Two years after the New York Giants had dropped such aging stars as Christy Mathewson, they were back on top in the National League, rising from last place in 1915 to the pennant. Newcomers Ferdie Schupp on the mound and hitters George Burns and Benny Kauff were instrumental in the Giants' 98 wins that year.

The Series opened on 6 October, and manager Clarence 'Pants' Rowland's White Sox took the first two games in Chicago. In the first game, Eddie Cicotte pitched a seven-hitter against Harry 'Slim' Sallee, 2-1. It was a thriller, the victory resting solely on a home run by Chicago center fielder Hap Felsh in the fourth inning. The second game was a little easier for the Sox, and they won it, 7-2, mainly because of the five runs they scored in the fourth inning. Urban 'Red' Faber was the victor over Fred Anderson, who had replaced Schupp in the second inning. Faber came close to being the goat of that game, however, when he tried to steal third base in the fifth inning after apparently forgetting that his teammate, shortstop Buck Weaver, was already occupying the bag.

The Giants and the White Sox went to New York for the next two games, and John McGraw's New York club staged a comeback. In the third game, which they won 2-0, pitcher Rube Benton threw a five-hitter at the Sox. The next day gave the fans another Giant shutout, as Schupp beat Faber, 5-0.

The fifth game in Chicago was a seesaw affair. Sox starter Reb Russell, who had won 15 games and lost but five during the season, was knocked out in less than one inning, when New York scored two runs. By the end of the seventh inning, the score was tied at five. Chicago scored three runs in the eighth to win the game, sending Sallee down to his second loss. The winning pitcher was Faber, who had come in to pitch the final two shutout innings.

The White Sox took the World Series in the sixth and final game, 5-0, but it could be argued that the Giants beat themselves. The game was scoreless going into the fourth inning, and then disaster struck. Chicago scored three runs on only two hits when Giant third baseman Heinie Zimmerman made a two-base error with a wild throw on Sox second baseman Eddie Collins, and right fielder Dave Robertson followed with a schoolboy muff of Joe Jackson's fly ball. Later, in a run-down, Zimmerman chased Collins over the plate, scoring a run, because catcher Bill Rariden and first baseman Walter Holke had left the plate uncovered, and Zimmerman had no place to throw. The winning pitcher was Eddie Cicotte and the loser was Rube Benton.

After the contest was over, Faber of the White Sox had become the seventh pitcher to win three games in a single World Series. Eddie Collins hit .409 and stole three bases – this was his twenty-sixth World Series game, a record up to that time. Robertson was the standout Giant of the Series, batting .500. The real goat of the Series was New York manager McGraw, who lost his fourth consecutive World Series.

LEFT: Chicago White Sox batboy Clarence Rowland Jr, son of Chicago's manager, on the field before the fourth game of the 1917 World Series.

'ABOVE: The Giants' southpaw Ferdie Schupp warms up before game two of the World Series. Schupp's 750 winning percentage led the league in 1917, but he lasted less than two innings in this game. His moment in the sun would come in game four, when he shut down the White Sox, 5-0.

RIGHT: Giant pitcher Rube Benton on the mound in the third game of the Series. Benton pitched a shutout, allowing only five hits – his team won on two runs.

1918

Boston Red Sox 4, Chicago Cubs 2

The baseball season of 1917 had begun shortly after the United States had entered World War I. Hank Gowdy of the Braves had been the first major-leaguer to enlist, but it was not until 1918 that baseball, classified as a 'nonessential industry,' began to feel the heat. General Enoch Crowder, the Provost Marshal, gave a 'work or fight' order that forced all draft age men to choose between the military and essential industries. By the 11 November 1918 Armistice many major-league players had been inducted into the armed forces, including such greats as Casey Stengel and Christy Mathewson. The major leagues were also ordered to suspend their seasons by Labor Day, and only the two championship clubs were permitted to extend their seasons in order to play the World Series.

The pennant winners were the Boston Red Sox and the Chicago Cubs, both of whom had lost many players to the armed services. The Cubs had bought the legendary pitcher, Grover Cleveland Alexander, from the Phillies the year before, but he was drafted early in the 1918 season. The Red Sox had lost such former World Series stars as Duffy Lewis, Jack Barry, Dutch Leonard, Dick Hoblitzell, Chick Shorten and others to the armed forces.

The first game of the Series was a white-knuckle contest. Manager Ed Barrow of the Sox picked Babe Ruth to pitch, and Fred Mitchell chose Jim Vaughn. Boston won the game, 1-0, on a run in the fourth inning in this duel between lefthanders. Chicago came back in the second game when George Tyler beat Joe Bush, 3-1. Tyler helped his own cause by singling in two runs in the second inning.

Vaughn was back in the third game against Carl Mays, but lost again, 2-1. The fourth game, one of the more interesting games in World Series history, was yet another one-run contest, as Boston came out on top, 3-2. Barrow had played Ruth in left field several times during the season, and the Babe had

RIGHT: Red Sox lefty Babe Ruth shut out the Cubs in game one of the 1918 Series and pitched a game four win as well, turning in a 1.06 Series ERA. The Babe's record scoreless inning streak, dating back to the 1916 Series, was stopped in the eighth inning of game four after 29.2 innings. Following two 20-win seasons, Ruth went 13 and 7 in 1918, while leading the league in hitting home runs, with 11.

LEFT: The Cubs' Fred Merkle is out at third in the ninth inning of the Series' fourth game. The Cubs lost the game by one run.

tied for the home run lead with 11. In this Series game, Ruth was sent in to relieve starting pitcher Bush, and went on to pitch seven and one-third scoreless innings before Chicago scored two runs in the eighth inning to tie the score. Boston countered with the go-ahead run in the bottom of the eighth, then Ruth was sent into left field, and was replaced on the mound by Joe Bush, who shut out the Cubs in the ninth. Until the Cubs scored, Ruth had run up a string of 29 and two-thirds consecutive scoreless World Series innings – a record that was not broken until 1961. Ruth, of course, was the winning pitcher over Phil Douglas.

There was a sit-down strike before game five. For the first time in history, the second-, third-, and fourth-place teams were to receive a share in the receipts, and the Cubs and Sox players, demanding larger shares, called the strike, thus delaying the

game for a time before they capitulated. The Cubs then won the game, 3-0, with Vaughn beating Sad Sam Jones. The sixth game handed the championship to the Red Sox, 4-2, as Mays beat Tyler, 2-1.

During the Series the hitting was extremely light – the Sox batting .186 against .210 for the Cubs. But the fielding was brilliant, with Boston making but one error in six games. The batting leaders were Charlie Pick, the Cubs' second baseman, with .389, and Sox catcher Wally Schang, with .444, although he had only nine times at bat. The star of the Series, however, was George Whiteman, an aging left fielder from Toronto, whom the Sox had picked up in midseason. His fielding and hitting helped Boston in all six games. In the Series-winning game, his hit gave the Red Sox the winning run in their 2-1 victory, and his spectacular catch in the eighth inning stopped a Cub rally dead.

1919

Cincinnati Reds 5, Chicago White Sox 3

The year 1919 stands out in baseball history, but not for good reasons. The Chicago White Sox, who had won the American League pennant in 1917, came back from their 1918 sixth-place finish to win the pennant easily under manager Kid Gleason. But no one knew that three of the Sox players, Eddie Cicotte, Arnold 'Chick' Gandil and Claude 'Lefty' Williams, had approached gamblers (including the notorious Arnold Rothstein) in New York at midseason to discuss a fix.

The Cincinnati Reds under manager Pat Moran won their first National League pennant by beating out the New York Giants by nine games. This faceoff created an enormous amount of interest, especially in the Midwest, and the National Commission voted to increase the length of the Series from the best four out of seven games to the best five out of nine. The players were to receive a share of the receipts of the first five games. But what should have been one of the greatest of all Series turned into the blackest chapter in major-league baseball history.

The White Sox, unquestionably one of the greatest teams of all time, were hands-down favorites to take the Series, but they were upset by the Reds by five games to three. Obviously, there were people who knew that the fix was on, since even before the Series started, the odds went from 3-1 White Sox to 8-5 Reds.

It was alleged that the prearranged signal from the players to the gamblers was to have the White Sox pitcher hit the first batter in the first game. Eddie Cicotte performed on cue, and the game turned into a rout, with Cincinnati winning, 9-1, behind Walter 'Dutch' Reuther. Cicotte was the loser.

There are those who feel that after that first game, the Series was played more or less on merit. Nevertheless, Cincinnati won the second game, 4-2, with Harry Sallee beating Claude Williams. In this game, Williams walked three batters in a single inning, an unheard-of feat for him.

The White Sox won the third game, 3-0, and there were those who later thought that that was because the gamblers were going back on their promise to pay the crooked players $10,000 of the $100,000 total after each game. Chicago pitcher Dickie Kerr threw a three-hitter to beat Ray Fisher. Cicotte was the Chicago pitcher in the fourth game, and the Reds won, 2-0, after he made two errors on the mound.

When Cincinnati won the fifth game in a 5-0 shutout in which Hod Eller struck out six Sox in a row to beat Williams, the Reds had a commanding four games to one lead in the Series. But then the Sox came back in the sixth game, when Kerr, although allowing 11 hits, beat Jimmy Ring, 5-4.

Cicotte prevailed on manager Gleason to let him pitch the seventh game and he came through this time, beating Sallee, 4-1. The eighth game was a disaster for Chicago. Cincinnati launched a 16-hit attack, winning 10-5 as Eller won his second game against a parade of Chicago pitchers. Williams took his third loss, and the Reds won the World Series five games to three.

It took almost a year for the game fixing to become general knowledge, although White Sox owner Charles Comiskey heard about it after the second game. When he passed the word to John Heydler, the president of the National League, Heydler informed Ban Johnson, the president of the American League. Johnson and Comiskey were

ABOVE: Chicago's Oscar 'Happy' Felsh (right) and 'Shoeless' Joe Jackson were both suspended from baseball forever by Commissioner Landis for their involvement in the Black Sox scandal.

OPPOSITE TOP: The 1919 White Sox pose for a team photo. Eight players were named by Boxer Abe Attell as being in on the Series fix.

OPPOSITE BOTTOM: The Reds' Heinie Groh scores as Pat Duncan rounds third base in the second game of the Series, which the Reds won, 4-2.

LEFT: Chicago pitchers Eddie Cicotte and Claude 'Lefty' Williams were involved in the Series fix. Cicotte lost two of the three Series games he pitched, while Williams lost all three Series games he pitched.

RIGHT: White Sox Buck Weaver is out at the plate in the second game of the 1919 World Series.

feuding at the time, and Johnson passed off the accusation as 'the yelp of a beaten cur.'

Nothing was said publicly about the fix until the following September, but rumors flew fast and furious. Boxer Abe Attell confessed to being involved in the deal and named eight players on a list of the guilty parties. The 'Black Sox' on the list were left fielder 'Shoeless Joe' Jackson, third baseman George 'Buck' Weaver, first baseman Arnold 'Chick' Gandil, shortstop Charles 'Swede' Risberg, pitchers Eddie Cicotte and Claude 'Lefty' Williams, center fielder Oscar 'Happy' Felsch and utility infielder Fred McMullin. Cicotte, Gandil and Williams were the ringleaders, and *The Chicago Tribune* called for a grand jury investigation.

When confronted by Gleason and Comiskey, Cicotte broke down. He, Jackson and Williams gave details of how the games were rigged to a grand jury, and Comiskey suspended all eight players, although some argued that Weaver was guilty only by association. He had sat in on the negotiations over the fix, but decided not to participate in it. As Jackson was leaving the courthouse after the grand jury hearing, a small boy supposedly came up to him with tears in his eyes, and, as legend has it, cried, 'Say it ain't so, Joe.' Criminal indictments followed, but by then the players' written confessions had disappeared, and they were all acquitted. According to the letter of the law, they could have been reinstated.

The three-man National Commission was replaced that year, however, by a single commissioner of baseball. Judge Kenesaw Mountain Landis took quick and decisive action. 'Regardless of the verdict of juries, no player that throws a game, no player that entertains proposals or promises to throw a game, no player that sits in conference with a bunch of crooks and gamblers where the ways and means of throwing games are discussed, and does not promptly tell his club about it, will ever again play professional baseball.'

The scandal of the 'Black Sox' seriously undermined the confidence of many in the game that had become the national pastime, but Landis' firm handling of the situation helped mitigate the disgrace. Some people felt that some of the players deserved a pardon. Buck Weaver never shared in the ill-gotten profits and batted .324 in the Series. Ten thousand fans signed a petition calling for his reinstatement, but Judge Landis sternly turned a cold shoulder.

Shoeless Joe Jackson got no fix money either, and averaged .375 for the Series, the highest average on either team, but he was never allowed back in baseball. In fact, when word got out to Landis that Jackson had been hired to coach a Class D minor-league team, he ordered him fired. It took the legendary Babe Ruth to wipe the slate clean in the roaring twenties and make the crowds forget about the dirty deeds their heroes in Chicago had done.

1920

Cleveland Indians 5, Brooklyn Dodgers 2

The year 1920 ushered in some major changes besides the installation of Kenesaw Mountain Landis as baseball commissioner. Trick pitches such as the spitball were outlawed, although pitchers who used the spitter were to be allowed to use it until the end of their careers. The lively ball came in, resulting in more hits and more runs.

That year, spurred on by spitballer Burleigh Grimes' 23 wins and the hitting of veteran left fielder Zack Wheat, Wilbert 'Uncle Robbie' Robinson's Brooklyn Dodgers took their second National League pennant in five years. After fighting off a strong late season threat by the New York Giants, they ended up eight games in front of the league.

A Cleveland Indian team powered by playing manager Tris Speaker's .388 batting average and pitcher Jim Bagby's 31 victories took the American League pennant, surviving a tight three-cornered race with the Yankees and the White Sox. The Indians finished two games ahead of Chicago, as the Sox saw most of their stars suspended because of the Black Sox scandal as the season progressed. The Yankees ended three games behind in third place.

The first game of the World Series really was never in doubt after Cleveland scored two runs in the second inning and one in the fourth. It ended 3-1 Cleveland, with Stanley Coveleski beating Rube Marquard. Brooklyn came back in the second game, 3-0, as Grimes beat Bagby. Then it was Brooklyn again, 2-1, with Sherry Smith defeating Ray Caldwell in a three-hitter. The fourth game saw Cleveland tying the Series by winning, 5-1. Pitching his second straight five-hit victory, Coveleski beat Leon Cadore.

The fifth game was monumental. First of all, the Indians' right fielder Elmer Smith hit the first grand slam home run in Series history. Cleveland pitcher Bagby hit the first World Series home run by a pitcher. And

RIGHT: Cleveland's ace pitcher and future Hall of Famer, Stan Coveleski, warms up before game one of the 1920 World Series. After pitching his way to a 24-14 record during the regular season, Coveleski won all three Series games he pitched – including a game seven shutout – and registered a 0.67 Series ERA.

OPPOSITE: Cleveland's second baseman Bill Wambsganss performed an unassisted triple play in the fifth inning of game five of the 1920 Series. Wambsganss caught Clarence Mitchell's line drive, stepped on second base before Pete Kilduff could get back, and tagged Otto Miller, running from first on the pitch.

BELOW: Indian outfielder Tris Speaker (right) with Cy Young before the Series' sixth game.

the Indians' second baseman Bill Wambsganss made the first Series unassisted triple play. Pete Kilduff was on second and Otto Miller was on first, and they were both running on Brooklyn pitcher Clarence Mitchell's line drive. Running to cover second, Wambsganss caught the line drive, stepped on second to retire Kilduff, and tagged Miller, who was coming in from first. The game ended with Cleveland winning 8-1, Bagby the winner and Grimes the loser.

Apparently the Dodgers were demoralized, since they didn't score a run in the last two games that Cleveland won to take the Series, five games to two. In the sixth game Walter 'Duster' Mails, a Dodger castoff, beat Smith 1-0 by scattering seven hits. And in the seventh game, the astonishing Coveleski turned in his third five-hitter to win his third Series game – 3-0 over Grimes.

1921

New York Giants 5, New York Yankees 3

In 1921 the World Series was played for the first time under the administration of Baseball Commissioner Kenesaw Mountain Landis. For the first time it was truly a 'subway series,' since both teams came from New York. The Yankees won the American League pennant in Babe Ruth's second year with the club, after he had come from the Boston Red Sox. He had hit 59 home runs, had knocked out 204 hits, and had batted in 170 runs. Ruth also carried an .846 slugging average, scored 177 runs and walked 144 times. The Giants finished in first place in the National League four games ahead of the second-place Pittsburgh Pirates.

The Yankees' Carl Mays, who had won 27 games that year, faced the Giants' Phil Douglas in the first game of the Series. Although the Giants' third baseman, Frankie Frisch, went four for four in the game, Miller Huggins' Yankees topped the Giants, 3-0. The Yankees won the second tilt, 3-0, with Waite Hoyt beating Art Nehf, although Nehf gave up but three hits, as did Hoyt.

John McGraw's Giants caught fire in the third game, winning it 13-5 after breaking a 4-4 tie in the seventh with eight runs. Jessie Barnes was the winner and Jack Quinn was the loser. The fourth game saw the Giants win again, but not so spectacularly. The contest ended at 4-2, with Douglas beating Mays.

The fifth game was decisive, but not because of its outcome. Nehf lost his second game to Hoyt as the Yankees won, 3-1. But the significance of the game was that Ruth was lost to the Yankees after the game because of an infected arm and a wrenched knee. In the Series he had hit .313, had drawn five walks, and had stolen second and third in succession in the second game.

Now leading three games to two, the Yankees proceeded to drop the next three games and lose the Series. In the sixth game Barnes beat Bob Shawkey, 8-5. The seventh game was won by Douglas over Mays, 2-1.

LEFT: In the 1921 Series' first game, Giant Ross Youngs hits to pitcher Carl Mays while Frankie Frisch, who went four for four in the game, starts toward second. Mays' underhand delivery baffled the Giants, who were shut out, 3-0.

ABOVE: The Giants' shortstop Dave Bancroft at bat in game two of the 1921 Series. Shut down for the second game in a row, the Giants lost, 3-0, on a Waite Hoyt two-hitter.

The eighth was a pitching duel between Nehf and Hoyt, with Nehf winning, 1-0, on the Giants' single run in the top of the first inning. The final – Giants, five games to three.

Despite the fact that he was on the losing side, the hero of the Series was probably Waite Hoyte, who had won 19 games during the regular season. In the World Series, he won two games and lost one. He had given up only two runs and both of them were unearned. This tied him with Christy Mathewson who, in 1905, pitched 27 innings in one Series without yielding an earned run.

1922

New York Giants 4, New York Yankees 0, 1 tie

The World Series went back to the old plan of best four out of seven in 1922. And the same two teams were back at the party – the Yankees and the Giants of New York.

Yankee slugging enabled the team to take the pennant, but it had been a close race, with the Bronx Bombers finishing only one game ahead of the St Louis Browns. In the National League, the Giants finished a comfortable seven games ahead of the Cincinnati Reds.

The Yankees were once again frustrated in the Series, however, suffering their second straight defeat at the hands of the Giants. The 1922 loss was even more devastating than the previous year's, with the Yankees managing only one tie in five games. The first game was a squeaker. With the Yankees leading 2-0, the Giants scored three runs in the bottom of the eighth inning to take the game, 3-2, with Wilfred 'Rosy' Ryan the winner in relief over Joe Bush.

The second game ended in a 3-3 tie in which Bob Shawkey of the Giants and Jess Barnes of the Yankees each gave up eight hits. There was quite a rhubarb after the game. The game was called at the end of the tenth inning on account of darkness by George Hildebrand, the home plate umpire. Since there was still about a half hour of light remaining, many of the fans were understandably upset and, possibly thinking that Commissioner Kenesaw Mountain Landis was the one who made the decision, some fans followed him with a chorus of boos as he made his way across the field. As a result of the disorder that followed, Landis ordered the receipts of the game to be turned over to New York charities.

The Giants won the third game, 3-0, behind the pitching of John Scott, who threw a four-hitter to beat Waite Hoyte. In the fourth game the Giants won, 4-3, with Hugh McQuillan beating Carl Mays. The fifth game was another heartbreaker for the Yankees, since they lost the game, 5-3, in a similar manner to the way

LEFT: A Giant run scores and the runner is safe at third during exciting 1922 Series action.

ABOVE: The Giants' Heinie Groh reaches third on his third-inning triple in the 1922 Series' first game. Groh's three for three performance helped his team to a 3-2 win.

RIGHT: Yankee Babe Ruth takes a mighty cut in the 1922 Series. Ruth had an atypically poor Series, batting .118.

they had lost the first game. The Yankees scored once in the first, the Giants twice in the second, and the Yanks once each in the fifth and seventh innings. Then came the fateful bottom of the eighth again, and the Giants scored three. The winner was Art Nehf and the loser was Joe Bush. It was the Giants, four games to none, with one tie.

Perhaps one of the main reasons for the Yankee failure was the collapse of Babe Ruth, who managed only one single and one double in 17 times at bat, for an average of .118. Then, too, the Giants outhit the

Yankees .309 to .203. Undoubtedly the heroes of the Series were Giants Heinie Groh and Frankie Frisch, who hit .474 and .471.

After the Series was over, Yankee half-owner Colonel T L Huston was so disgusted at the play of his team that he called for the dismissal of manager Miller Huggins, a move that widened the rift between Huston and co-owner Jacob Ruppert. Ruppert refused to consider letting Huggins go, and over the winter Huston sold out to Ruppert, who became the sole owner of the team.

1923

New York Yankees 4, New York Giants 2

It was the Yankees and the Giants once again in the World Series of 1923. This time the Yanks rewarded their owner, Jacob Ruppert, with a four game to two championship in the first Series ever played in 'The House That Ruth Built' – the brand new Yankee Stadium. The Yankees had few problems during the season, winning their third straight pennant by a margin of 16 games over the Detroit Tigers. The Giants, on the other hand, had been in a dogfight, and finished only four and a half games ahead of the Cincinnati Reds. One sidelight of the end of the season was that Yankee first baseman Wally Pipp sprained his ankle, but Giant manager John McGraw refused to let the Yankees replace him in the Series with a young ballplayer who had been recalled from Hartford of the Eastern League – a young man named Lou Gehrig. Still, the taped-up Pipp played good ball in the Series and batted .250.

The first game of the Series was a thriller, with the Giants winning 5-4, with Wilfred 'Rosy' Ryan defeating Joe Bush. The hero of the game was the Giants' center fielder Casey Stengel. With the game tied 4-4 in the top of the ninth inning, he made the game-winning hit – an inside-the-park home run.

The Yankees came back in the second game, winning 4-2, with Herb Pennock outpitching Hugh McQuillan. The third game gave Stengel another chance to star. Art Nehf of the Yankees and Sad Sam Jones of the Yankees were engaged in a real pitchers' duel when Casey hit a seventh inning belt into the right field bleachers and the Giants won, 1-0. In the fourth game the Yankee hitters began to go to work. Bob Shawkey pitched the Yankees to an 8-4 victory over Jack Scott, as the Bronx Bombers pounded out 13 hits.

The Yanks came back with 14 hits to win the fifth game, 8-1, as Joe Bush beat Jack Bentley on a three-hitter, with all of them being hit by Giant left fielder Emil Meusel. Then came the sixth game and the Yankees' big offensive inning. Art Nehf of the Giants was comfortably ahead of Herb Pennock and the

LEFT: Bob Meusel scores the third Yankee run in the first inning of the 1923 Series' fifth game. The Yanks scored early and often in this game, putting four runs across the plate in the second inning as well.

OPPOSITE TOP: Yankee Wally Schang is caught between third and home in the fourth inning of game one, which the Yanks would lose by one run.

OPPOSITE BOTTOM: The Giants' Casey Stengel slides home safely with a game-winning inside-the-park homer in the 1923 Series' first game. Stengel batted .417 in the Series, with two home runs.

Yankees, 4-1. Then, after two hits and two walks in the eighth inning, Nehf was relieved by Ryan, who walked another man. When Bob Meusel hit a single that bounced over the pitcher's head, the game was lost. The Yankees scored five runs and went on to win, 6-4. The Series was over.

Ruth was the hero of the Series. He hit .368, with three homers (two in succession in the second game), a triple, a double and three singles. He also walked eight times. Oddly enough, the new Yankee Stadium was not all that lucky for the Yankees. The Yanks won all three games at the Giants' Polo Grounds, but won only one out of three at the Stadium.

1924

Washington Senators 4, New York Giants 3

The Washington Senators took their first American League pennant in 1924, preventing the Yankees from winning four pennants in a row by a two-game margin. The Giants were back again after winning the National League championship by one and a half games over the Brooklyn Dodgers.

In the first game, the great pitching legend, Walter Johnson, was the starter for the Senators, and was getting his first World Series start in his 18 seasons with the club. Facing him was Art Nehf. Although Johnson had had a 23-7 record that season, he was bombed in the Series opener. New York lashed him for 14 hits to win the game, 4-3, in 12 innings. The second game was won by Washington, 4-3, when they scored a run in the bottom of the ninth to break the tie. Tom Zachary was the winner and Jack Bentley the loser.

The Giants came back in the third game, winning it 6-4 behind Hugh McQuillan. The loser was Fred Marberry. In the fourth game, the Senators again evened things up by winning it 7-4, with George Mogridge defeating Virgil Barnes. Once again the Giants went ahead, taking the fifth game 6-2, scoring three runs in the bottom of the eighth inning, Bentley winning and Johnson again losing. The sixth game tied the Series up once again as the Senators won by a score of 2-1 behind Zachary, who beat Nehf.

Then came the wild and thrilling final game of the Series. Things were looking rosy for the Giants as they had scored three runs in the sixth inning to take a 3-1 lead. The championship was in their grasp. But then came the fateful eighth inning. Washington second baseman and boy manager, the 28-year-old Stanley 'Bucky' Harris, hit a grounder to third baseman Fred Lindstrom that bounced over Lindstrom's head. There were two men on base at the time, and both of them scored, tying the game. With the score still tied in the ninth inning, Walter Johnson, who so far had had a terrible Series, was sent in to pitch. He held on for four

LEFT: The Senators' veteran ace, Hall of Famer Walter Johnson. After racking up amazing stats for 18 seasons with the club, Johnson finally got to pitch in a World Series in 1924. 'The Big Train' fanned 12 but lost game one after 12 innings, pitched another losing effort in game five, but clinched the Series for Washington in relief in game seven.

OPPOSITE TOP: The sixth game of the 1924 Series tied Washington and the Giants at three games each, as the Senators' southpaw Tom Zachary beat Art Nehf, 2-1.

OPPOSITE BOTTOM: Washington's Goose Goslin is out on a close play at first after hitting to Giant shortstop Travis Jackson in the second inning of the 1924 Series' game one.

gruelling innings, giving up a mere three hits and striking out five. In the bottom of the twelfth inning, Giant catcher Hank Gowdy caught his foot in his mask while trying to catch Washington catcher Herold 'Muddy' Ruel's routine foul fly. Ruel's life at bat was saved and he promptly hit a double – only his second hit of the Series. Then Earl McNeely, the Senators' center fielder, hit another ball to Lindstrom. Once again the ball took a bad hop, and the Senators had won the Series four games to three. Bentley was the loser and the legendary Johnson finally had a World Series victory.

1925

Pittsburgh Pirates 4, Washington Senators 3

As the National League began its fiftieth season in 1925, the Pittsburgh Pirates moved up from their fifth place berth in 1924 to take the pennant and end the Giants' four-year reign, with an eight-and-a-half-game bulge over New York. Washington repeated easily that year, also finishing eight and a half games ahead of their nearest rival – the Philadelphia Athletics. The 1925 World Series turned out to be one of the most exciting of all time.

Walter Johnson had turned in a 20-7 season that year, his last 20-game year, and of course he was the pitcher for the Senators in the opener. He gave up only five hits in beating Lee Meadows, 4-1. In the second game it was spitballer Stanley Coveleski who started for the Washington club – he had been obtained from Cleveland that year, and had turned in his fifth consecutive 20-game record. But the Pirates beat this hero of the World Series five years before, winning, 3-2, behind Vic Aldridge.

Ray Kremer of the Pirates faced Alex Ferguson of the Senators in the third game, which Washington won, 4-3. The fourth game was another triumph for Johnson, who beat the Pirate relief pitcher Emil Yde, 4-0, by scattering six hits. Now the Pirates were trailing in the Series three games to one, and to get his team going, Pittsburgh manager Bill McKechnie benched first baseman George Grantham and inserted veteran John 'Stuffy' McInnis, who became the sparkplug of the team.

In the fifth game, Aldridge hung on to beat Coveleski, 6-3. Then the Pirates came back again in a 3-2 squeaker of a sixth game behind Kremer, who defeated Ferguson. The Series was tied, three games to three.

The final game was a thriller. Johnson was back pitching for the Senators and faced Aldridge. Washington leaped off to a four-run lead in the top of the first inning. Then Pittsburgh scored three runs in the third. In the fourth, Washington went farther ahead with two runs, and the Pirates answered with another one in

RIGHT: Senator Ossie Bluege is safe at home on a Roger Peckinpaugh double in the second inning of the 1925 Series' game six. Pittsburgh would win this game, 3-2, to tie up the Series.

OPPOSITE TOP: Senator Joe Judge's game two homer was not enough, as the Pirates scored three runs on two home runs to take the game, 3-2.

FAR RIGHT: Baseball commissioner Judge Landis watches the Senators beat the Pirates, 4-1, in the 1925 Series opener.

the fifth. In the sixth inning, pitching hero Kremer came in to relieve and held on for the final four innings, giving up only one hit, a homer by Senator shortstop Roger Peckinpaugh. In the meantime, the Pirates scored two runs in the seventh and three in the eighth, banging out 15 hits in the game to win the Series and defeat Johnson, 9-7.

The Series had been as close as could be imagined. For example, the Pirates had a team batting average of .265 and the Senators hit .262. The Pirates had staged a comeback unparalleled in a seven-game Series, winning out after they were trailing three games to one.

1926

St Louis Cardinals 4, New York Yankees 3

In 1926 Babe Ruth came back strong, hitting 47 home runs and batting .372. Largely because of this, the Yankees won another American League pennant, edging out the Cleveland Indians by three games. In the National League, the St Louis Cardinals won their first pennant. That meant that every team in the National League had now won at least one flag. The city of St Louis had not come in first since the Browns won in 1888. Grover Cleveland Alexander, war-scarred and 39 years old, was the sparkplug of the team. He had been traded in the middle of the season to the Cardinals by the Chicago Cubs, who had thought he was burned out, but he won nine games for the Cards. Neither team had been a shoo-in for the championship – the Cardinals had won the pennant with a miserable winning percentage of .578, and the Yankees had posted a .591.

St Louis manager Rogers Hornsby nominated Willie Sherdel to pitch in the first game, and the Yankees' Miller Huggins picked Herb Pennock. It was a pitchers' duel, with the Yankees winning, 2-1. St Louis came back to tie the Series in the second game, as Alexander pitched a four-hitter to defeat Urban Shocker, 6-2. Alexander retired 21 Yankees in order.

Jess Haines pitched a five-hitter for the Cardinals to beat Walt Ruether, 4-0, in the third contest. The fourth game was a barnburner, with each team getting 14 hits. Ultimately, Waite Hoyt won the game for the Yankees, 10-5. Art Reinhart was the loser.

In the fifth tilt Sherdel lost again to Pennock in another pitchers' duel, 3-2, in ten innings. It was Alexander's turn again in the sixth game, and he scattered eight hits to beat starter Bob Shawkey of the Yankees, 10-2, winning his second complete game of the Series.

Now the Series was tied three games to three, and the stage was set for one of the most exciting final

LEFT: One of the most dramatic moments in World Series history occurred in game seven on 10 October 1926, as Yankee Tony Lazzeri was struck out by Cardinal Grover Cleveland Alexander with the bases loaded and two out. Alexander pitched two more hitless innings to save the Series for St Louis.

OPPOSITE TOP: Babe Ruth blasts the first of his record-setting three homers in one Series game, in the first inning of game four at Sportsman's Park.

OPPOSITE BOTTOM: St Louis' second baseman-manager Rogers Hornsby crosses the plate with the second run in the first inning of game six, at Yankee Stadium.

games in World Series history. Hoyt was the Yankee starter against Haines for the Cards. At the end of six innings, St Louis was ahead, 3-2. But in the seventh inning, the Yankees loaded the bases with two men out. Once again, Alexander was called to save the bacon. He walked to the mound and faced Tony 'Push 'Em Up' Lazzeri, the Yankee second baseman, who had finished the season in second place in the runs batted in category. Alexander struck him out in a clutch performance, and finished the final two innings without giving up a hit, saving the game for Haines and the Series for the Cards. The winner – St Louis, four games to three.

Babe Ruth had been a star in a losing cause, batting .300 and smashing four homers. But the Cinderella of the Series was St Louis shortstop, Tommy Thevenow, who had hit .265 during the regular season – in the Series he batted .417 to lead both clubs.

1927

New York Yankees 4, Pittsburgh Pirates 0

In 1927 the Yankees were so hot that there was virtually no pennant race. Considered by many to be the best team ever, the 1927 Yankees never fell from first place, and ended the season a league-record 19 games ahead of the second-place Philadelphia Athletics. Their 110 wins and .714 winning percentage remained the best in league history until Cleveland took the pennant in 1954. This was also the year that the legendary Babe Ruth reached his home run peak of 60 and Lou Gehrig – the Iron Horse – knocked in a record 175 runs.

Donie Bush's Pittsburgh Pirates won the National League pennant with a .305 team batting average. After a season-long struggle with the St Louis Cardinals, the New York Giants and the Chicago Cubs, they finally nosed out the Cards by one and a half games. The Pirates featured the hitting of the Waner brothers, Paul (Big Poison) and Lloyd (Little Poison). Paul had led the league with an average of .380 and the rookie Lloyd had hit .355.

The story goes that before the first game of the World Series, the Pirates came out as the Yankees were taking batting practice and were so awed by watching Babe Ruth, Lou Gehrig, Bob Meusel and Tony Lazzeri knock successive balls into the bleachers that they never recovered. The truth is that the Pirates beat themselves in the first game. Miller Huggins' New Yorkers won the contest, 5-4, Waite Hoyt defeating Ray Kremer. In the first inning, Paul Waner muffed a shoestring catch off a Gehrig fly to right field, and Gehrig had a run-producing triple. The Yanks picked up three runs in the third on errors by second baseman George Grantham and catcher Earl Smith. In the second game George Pipgras of the Yankees faced Ralph Dawson, and the New Yorkers won, 6-2. Game three was more humiliating for the Pirates as they lost again, 8-1, when Herb Pennock defeated Lee Meadows. Pennock's performance was a classic, as he retired 22

LEFT: The Yanks' Lou Gehrig flies out to center field in the fifth inning of the 1927 Series' second game, which New York won, 6-2. For the Series Gehrig batted five runs in on four hits – two doubles and two triples.

OPPOSITE TOP: A team photo of the 1927 Yankees – considered by many to be the best team ever. Miller Huggins' Bombers came out of the season with a .714 winning percentage.

OPPOSITE BOTTOM: Babe Ruth gets back to first after chopping a single in the Series' first game. This was one of three hits Ruth got that game to help his team win.

Pirates in a row before third baseman Pie Traynor singled in the eighth inning. This three-hitter was Pennock's fifth World Series victory against no defeats.

The fourth game saw the Pirates putting up a bit of a fight before going down to defeat, 4-3. The surprise starter for the Yanks was Wilcy Moore, who was usually a relief pitcher. He faced John Miljus. The Yankees were leading, 3-1, at the end of the sixth inning, and then the Pirates tied the game in the seventh. But in the ninth inning, Yankee center fielder Earle Combs and shortstop Mark Koenig beat out a bunt. Both of them advanced a base on a wild pitch, and Ruth was given an intentional pass. The bases were loaded with no one out, but Miljus struck out first baseman Gehrig and left fielder Bob Meusel. Then came the disaster. Miljus made his second wild pitch of the inning, and Combs scored. For the first time in history the American League representative had swept the World Series.

1928

New York Yankees 4, St Louis Cardinals 0

The Yankees repeated as American League champions in 1928, but not without a struggle. By early July they were 13 and a half games ahead of the pack, but ran into trouble when Tony Lazzeri, Joe Dugan, Bob Meusel, Herb Pennock and Mark Koenig were injured. But the Yanks came through when they had to, and edged out the Athletics by two and a half games.

The Cardinals returned to the winner's circle that year, but only after a fight. They didn't clinch the pennant until the next-to-the-last day of the season.

The Yanks were still crippled going into the Series. Pitcher Pennock was out with a lame arm, center fielder Earle Combs had a broken finger, second baseman Tony Lazzeri had a sore arm and right fielder Babe Ruth had a bad ankle. Bit it didn't seem to make any difference. In the Series, Ruth batted .625, still the highest batting average in World Series history, slugging three homers in one game. First baseman Lou Gehrig batted .545, hit four homers, drove in nine runs and scored five.

New York had no trouble in the first game, as Waite Hoyt beat Sylvester Johnson, 4-1, on a three-hitter. In the second game, the Yankees erupted for eight runs in the first three innings, and George Pipgras beat Grover Cleveland Alexander, 9-3, on a four-hitter. The Cards did a little better in the third game, scoring three runs, but still succumbed to the pitching of Tom Zachary, 7-3. The loser was Jesse Haines. The final game was won by the Yanks by an identical score, 7-3, with Hoyt the winner over Bill Sherdel.

New York had swept its second straight Series. Sam Breadon, the president of the Cardinals, was so disappointed at his team's pitiful showing after the Series that he sent his manager, Bill McKechnie, to manage Rochester in the minor leagues, bringing in Billy Southworth to replace him.

ABOVE: The Cardinals' manager, Bill McKechnie, in the dugout with his star pitcher, Grover Cleveland Alexander. Both are in the Hall of Fame.

OPPOSITE: The Yankee infield executes a double play in the seventh inning of game two, on their way to a 9-3 victory.

1929

Philadelphia Athletics 4, Chicago Cubs 1

The World Series of 1929 featured a new cast of characters. Under the managership of former minor-league infielder Joe McCarthy, the Chicago Cubs beat out the second-place Pittsburgh Pirates by 10 and a half games (this was the first of nine pennants for McCarthy with the Cubs and the Yankees) – the first championship for the Cubs since 1918. It was a hitting team. The Cubs' winning outfield of Kiki Cuyler, Hack Wilson and Riggs Stephenson batted .360, .345 and .362 respectively. Second baseman Rogers Hornsby hit 40 homers and batted in 149 runs for a .380 average.

The Philadelphia Athletics, who had almost won the American League pennant the year before, were unstoppable. Connie Mack's club took their first flag in 15 years, beating out the Yankees by 18 games.

Mack got off to a surprising start in the Series by using Howard Ehmke, who was not part of the regular starting pitching rotation. Ehmke kept the Cubs off-balance with his slow stuff, struck out 13 (a Series record that stood until 1953) and won, 3-1. Charlie Root was the losing pitcher. The Athletics won the second game quite convincingly as George Earnshaw (the winning pitcher) and Lefty Grove combined in another 13-strikeout game and beat Pat Malone, 9-3.

The Cubs came to life in the third game, winning 3-1 behind Guy Bush, with Earnshaw the loser. The fourth game started with Root facing John Quinn. After six and a half innings Chicago seemed to have the game in its pocket, with a commanding 8-0 lead. But in the bottom of the seventh the Athletics exploded with the most overwhelming one-inning display in World Series history. Fifteen men went to the plate and the A's scored 10 runs on a total of 10 hits, a walk and a hit batsman. Center fielder Mule Haas also hit an inside-the-park home run. The final score was 10-8, with the win going to reliever Ed Rommel and the loss to Fred Blake, the third of five pitchers used by the Cubs in the game.

LEFT: Mule Haas slides home after belting a seventh-inning, three-run homer to fire Philadelphia's ten-run rally in the 1929 Series' game four. The A's overcame an 8-0 deficit to beat the Cubs, 10-8.

ABOVE: For the first play of the 1929 Series, at Wrigley Field, Max Bishop grounds out to Cub first baseman Charlie Grimm.

The fifth game became another horror show for Chicago. With the Cubs leading 2-0 in the bottom of the ninth inning, Malone retired pinch–hitter Walter French. Then second baseman Max Bishop singled, and scored on another Haas home run that tied the score at 2-2. Malone then retired Mickey Cochrane, the catcher. With two out, left fielder Al Simmons doubled and first baseman Jimmy Foxx was given an intentional pass. The Cubs lost another Series when right fielder Bing Miller doubled to score Simmons for a 3-2 win. The winning pitcher was George Walberg and the loser was Malone. The Athletics had won the Series, four games to one.

ABOVE: Cub Hack Wilson, who batted .471 for the 1929 Series, strikes out in the sixth inning of game two. The A's went on to win the game, 9-3.

1930

Philadelphia Athletics 4, St Louis Cardinals 2

The 1930 Cardinals, featuring eight .300 hitters in their lineup and four more on the bench, finished two games ahead of the Chicago Cubs to take the National League pennant.

The Philadelphia Athletics repeated that year, winning the American League championship by finishing eight games ahead of the Washington Senators.

The first game pitted Bob Grove of the Athletics against Burleigh Grimes of the Cardinals. Grimes was the loser, and it was a tough game to drop. In the 5-2 Philadelphia triumph, the Cards outhit the Athletics nine hits to five, but all five of the A's hits were for extra bases – catcher Mickey Cochrane and left fielder Al Simmons hit home runs, first baseman Jimmy Foxx and center fielder Mule Haas hit triples, and third baseman Jimmy Dykes hit a double. And all of the five hits were good for a run.

George Earnshaw was to pitch magnificently in the Series, and he began in the second game, scattering six hits in a 6-1 Philadelphia triumph. The loser was Charles Rhem. St Louis started a comeback in the third game, in which southpaw Bill Hallahan threw a seven-hit shutout to beat George Walberg, 5-0. St Louis won again to tie the Series in the fourth game, Jess Haines pitching a four-hitter to beat Bob Grove, 3-1. That was the last win for manager Gabby Street's Cardinals.

The fifth game was a masterpiece of excitement. Earnshaw was pitted against Grimes, and they put on a real pitchers' exhibition. Both of them had bad luck. Earnshaw pitched shutout ball for the first seven innings and was then taken out for a pinch-hitter. Grove relieved him and was the eventual winner, when the Athletics scored twice in the ninth inning. On the other hand, Grimes had a five-hit loss in the 2-0 game.

The Athletics pulled the same stunt in the sixth game that they had done in the first. With Earnshaw facing Hallahan, the A's garnered seven hits – all of them for extra bases, and all resulted in runs. Philadelphia

LEFT: Team managers – the Cardinals' Gabby Street (left) and the Athletics' Connie Mack – shake hands before game one of the 1930 World Series. Mack's A's boasted a .662 winning percentage that year, compared with the Redbirds' .597.

OPPOSITE TOP: In the seventh inning of game two, the Athletics' Mule Haas steals home as Joe Boley bunts. The A's won this contest, 6-1.

OPPOSITE BOTTOM: Philadelphia puts the Series' sixth and final game away as Jimmy Dykes crosses the plate with the fifth Athletic run after banging a two-run round-tripper in the fourth inning. The A's scored seven runs on seven hits (all for extra bases) as the Cards squeezed one run out of five hits.

had won the game, 7-1, and the Series, four games to two. The pitching had been great, even in that year of the hitter. The Cards managed a pathetic team batting average of .200 and the A's were worse, with a .197. For Connie Mack, the win was his fifth world title, a record for a manager up to that date, but it was also to be his last, although he would manage the team for 20 more seasons.

1931

St Louis Cardinals 4, Philadelphia Athletics 3

This was the year in which manager Connie Mack won his ninth and last American League pennant. The Philadelphia Athletics had a sensational year, winning 107 games – the highest number they had ever won – and ending up with a winning percentage of .704, the second best ever in the American League. The leaders of the club were the legendary pitcher, Robert M 'Lefty' Grove, who won the league's Most Valuable Player Award [MVP] that year, and left fielder Al Simmons, who led the league with a batting average of .390. Grove had won an incredible 31 games, and lost but four. Of his four losses, three of them were by one run and the fourth by two runs. His earned run average was a minuscule 2.05. During the season there was a period in which he won 16 straight games.

The St Louis Cardinals, soon to be known as 'The Gashouse Gang,' featuring such colorful players as center fielder John 'Pepper' Martin, had an easy time, too, in winning the National League championship. They won 101 games and romped to the flag by a margin of 13 games ahead of the second-place New York Giants. The Series turned out to be a thriller.

Philadelphia won the first game, 6-2, as Grove scattered 12 hits. The game was never in doubt after the Athletics scored four runs in the third inning. The loser was rookie Paul Derringer, who gave up 11 hits. The next game went to the Cardinals, 2-0, as Bill Hallahan threw a three-hitter to defeat George Earnshaw. The third game saw the Redbirds win again, 5-2, although the A's gave them a scare when they scored their two runs in the bottom of the ninth inning. Spitballer Burleigh Grimes beat Grove in this one, on a magnificent two-hitter.

Philadelphia came back to even the Series in the fourth game, 3-0. This time it was Earnshaw's turn to toss a two-hitter, and he beat Syl Johnson. The Cards went ahead three games to two in the fifth game, win-

LEFT: Jim Bottomly of the Cardinals is forced out at second during game five of the 1931 Series, which St Louis went on to win, defeating Philadelphia, 5-1.

ABOVE: The Cards' Pepper Martin slides home safely in the eighth inning of game two. With two hits and two stolen bases, Martin scored the Cards' only two runs in support of Bill Hallahan's shutout.

ning 5-1 as Hallahan scattered nine hits. Former Yankee Waite Hoyt took the loss. The sixth game saw the Series knotted again, as Grove beat Derringer with a complete game victory, 8-1.

The final game was won by the Cardinals, but not without a struggle. Grimes had blanked the Athletics for eight straight innings, but had to be relieved in the ninth, when Philadelphia scored two runs and had the tying run on base. Hallahan came in to relieve, and the A's failed to score. The 4-2 game ended with Earnshaw the loser, and the Cards had a four games to three world championship.

The hero of the Series was unquestionably the rookie Pepper Martin. He stole five bases and had 12 hits, including four doubles and one home run, for a .500 average. He scored five runs and batted in five, including four in the fifth game.

1932

New York Yankees 4, Chicago Cubs 0

This was the year of Joe McCarthy's revenge. He had been dismissed as the manager of the Chicago Cubs late in the 1930 season. Now he was the manager of the New York Yankees, and revenge was sweet. At the end of the 1932 season, the Yanks were in first place, having won 107 games and finishing 13 games ahead of the previous year's American League champions, the Philadelphia Athletics. Charlie 'Jolly Cholly' Grimm was appointed the manager of the Cubs toward the end of the season, and he guided them to the National League pennant, although with a lackluster .584 winning percentage – ahead of the Pittsburgh Pirates by four games. The Series could only be described as a debacle.

Guy Bush of the Cubs faced Red Ruffing of the Yankees in the first game, and for three innings it looked good for Chicago, since they scored two runs in the top of the first. Then the Yankees scored three runs in the fourth, five runs in the sixth, three runs in the seventh and one run in the eighth to win, 12-6 – all this on a mere 10 hits. The second game was a little closer, with the Yankees winning only 5-2, with Lefty Gomez beating Lon Warneke, but giving up 10 hits to nine.

The Cubs looked a little better in the third game, even being able to tie it up, 4-4, in the fourth inning. But the Yankees went on to win it, 7-5, with George Pipgras beating Charlie Root. It was in this game that a historic event took place – perhaps an apocalyptic one. In the fifth inning, with the score tied, Babe Ruth came to bat and, it is said, pointed to the most distant part of Wrigley Field with his bat. It looked as though he took two deliberate strikes from Root, and then hit a homer into the section of the bleachers to which he had pointed. Lou Gehrig followed with a homer (both Gehrig and Ruth hit two home runs in this game), and the Cubs' doom was sealed.

Chicago fans were cheered for a time in the fourth game when the Cubs scored four runs in the first

LEFT: In the fourth inning of the 1932 Series' game two, Cub catcher Gabby Hartnett runs down Earle Combs and doubles up Joe Sewell at third for a twin killing. The Yankees went on to win, 5-2.

ABOVE: A Robert Thom painting depicts Babe Ruth's famous 'called shot,' when he allegedly pointed to the fence in game three, then blasted a home run to the same spot.

ABOVE: The Cubs' first baseman, Charlie Grimm, at bat in the first game of the 1932 Series. The Cubs lost this game to the Bronx Bombers, 12-6.

LEFT: Lou Gehrig slides home safely on a third-inning single by Ben Chapman, which gave New York the lead in game two. Gehrig scored two runs on three hits as the Yankees beat the Cubs, 5-2.

inning to go ahead by a score of 4-1. Then the Yankees began to apply their version of the Chinese water torture by scoring two runs in the third, two in the sixth, four in the seventh and four in the ninth. The final score was 13-6, and the winner was Wilcy Moore. Frank May was the unfortunate loser, but he was merely one of five Cub pitchers used in the game, although he was almost com-

pletely ineffective. In the three and one-third innings he pitched, he gave up eight hits, three walks and hit Gehrig with a pitch.

The star of the Series was Lou Gehrig. Larrupin' Lou batted .529, getting nine hits, including three homers and a double, walked twice, was hit once, scored nine runs and drove in eight. The Cubs, who lost four games to none, were never in the Series.

1933

New York Giants 4, Washington Senators 1

In their first full season under new manager Bill Terry, the New York Giants moved into first place on 10 June 1933 and led the National League the rest of the way, finishing five games ahead of the Pittsburgh Pirates. Part of the credit went to Carl Hubbell – the 'Meal Ticket' – who won 23 games, 10 of them shutouts (including 46 straight innings of no-run pitching), and finished with an amazing 1.66 earned run average. Player-manager Joe Cronin, directing the team from his shortstop position, led the Washington Senators to the American League flag with 99 wins. They finished seven games ahead of the New York Yankees.

In the first game of the World Series, the Giants scored two runs in the first inning and two in the third, and that was all they needed as Carl Hubbell beat Walter Stewart, 4-2. For the first five innings of the second game, the fans watched a white-knuckler, as the Senators scored once in the third and held on for two more innings. Then the Giants accumulated six in the sixth, and the final score was 6-1, with Hal Schumacher beating Alvin Crowder on a five-hitter.

Washington came back in the third game, winning it 4-0. Earl Whitehill threw a five-hitter at losing pitcher Fred Fitzsimmons. The fourth game was the first really exciting game of the Series. For 10 innings it was a real pitchers' duel, with Hubbell battling with Monty Weaver in a 1-1 contest. But then came the eleventh inning, and New York scored a run on a bunt single by Travis Jackson, a sacrifice and a single. In the bottom of the inning Senator pinch-hitter Cliff Bolton hit into a double play with the bases loaded and one out, to give New York the cliffhanger, 2-1.

The Senators were still hopeful in the fifth game. The Giants scored two runs in the second inning and one in the sixth. But the never-say-die Washingtonians came back in the bottom of the sixth to tie the game at 3-3. Giant pitcher Schumacher was knocked out in that inning by center fielder Fred Schulte's three-run homer, and Senator pitcher Alvin 'General' Crowder was replaced by reliever Jack Russell. Both of the relievers hung on, Russell giving up four hits and the Giants' Adolfo Luque giving up two. Then in the tenth inning, right fielder Mel Ott made the Giants the world champions with a home run. New York had won the game, 4-3, and the Series four games to one.

LEFT: The New York Giants' player-manager Bill Terry autographs a baseball before the first game of the 1933 World Series. The Giants won three pennants during the 10 years they were skippered by 'Memphis Bill,' who was elected to the Hall of Fame in 1954.

OPPOSITE TOP: The grandstand and bleachers of New York's Polo Grounds were crowded as the New York Giants hosted the Washington Senators in the first game of the 1933 World Series.

OPPOSITE BOTTOM: Giant Kiddo Davis scores on Gus Mancuso's double in the sixth inning of the 1933 Series' fifth and final game. The Senators came back in the bottom of the inning to tie up the game with a three-run homer, but in the tenth inning Mel Ott's homer gave New York the championship.

1934

St Louis Cardinals 4, Detroit Tigers 3

In 1934 the Detroit Tigers took their first pennant in 25 years, a win that marked the first time a club outside the Eastern Division had taken the American League flag since Cleveland in 1920. The club was sparked by player-manager Mickey Cochrane (a catcher) and pitchers Lynwood 'Schoolboy' Rowe (who won 24 games) and Tommy Bridges (a 22-game winner).

In the National League, Frankie Frisch's Cardinals beat out the New York Giants on the last day of the season, finishing two games in front. The two Dean brothers, Dizzy and Daffy, had made pitching history that year. Jay Hanna Dean (Dizzy) had won 30 games and the younger Paul (Daffy) triumphed in 19. And the rest of the Gashouse Gang was in fine form.

The first game of the World Series was a rather sloppy one, with the Cardinals winning by a score of 8-3. By the time that the Tigers scored their first run, St Louis was already ahead by three runs. Then, when the Tigers scored their second run, St Louis was ahead by seven runs. In addition, the Tigers committed five errors as Dizzy Dean beat Alvin Crowder. Detroit snapped out of the doldrums in the second game, winning it 3-2 in a come-from-behind contest, with Rowe defeating Cardinal reliever Bill Walker, who had replaced Bill Hallahan in the ninth inning with the score tied, 2-2. Rowe held the Cards to a mere seven hits in twelve innings.

St Louis went ahead once again in the third game, winning it 4-1 behind Paul Dean, who outpitched Tom Bridges. After six innings the score in the fourth game was tied at 4-4. Then the Tigers scored one run in the seventh and erupted for five more in the eighth to win, 10-4, behind Elden Auker. The Series was tied again. Walker was the losing pitcher and Dizzy Dean made an appearance as a pinch-runner for Virgil Davis, who was hit on the head by Tiger shortstop Billy Rogell and had to be carried from the field.

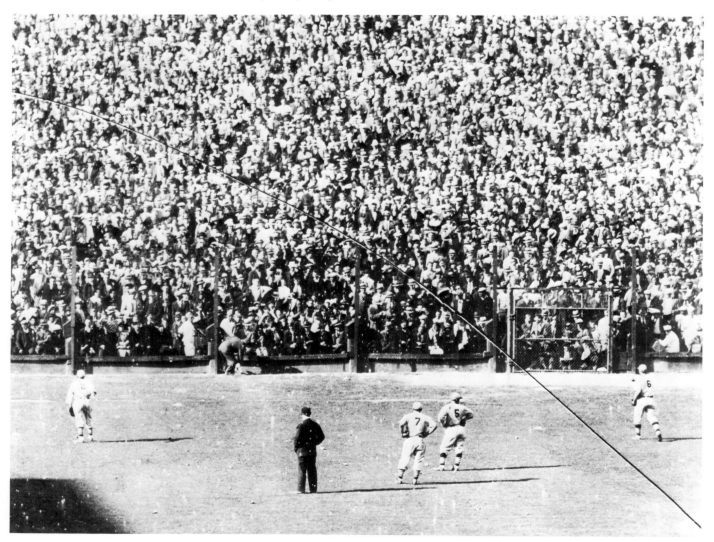

LEFT: Game seven in Detroit is delayed while the field is cleared of vegetables and debris thrown by Tiger fans at Cardinal Ducky Medwick, who had slid aggressively into third baseman Marv Owen. Medwick was removed from the game for his own safety.

ABOVE: Cardinal pitcher Paul 'Daffy' Dean in action during game six. Dean beat the Tigers, 4-3, for his second win in the 1934 Series.

RIGHT: Tiger slugger Charlie Gehringer crosses the plate after hitting a sixth-inning home run — which proved to be the game-winner — in game five. Gehringer finished the season with a league-leading 214 hits and a .356 batting average, then batted .379 in the Series.

The Tigers won the fifth game, 3-1, in a pitching duel between Bridges, who was working on a day of rest, and Dizzy Dean. Then in the sixth game St Louis tied the Series in another one-run game by a score of 4-3. Paul Dean was the victor over Rowe.

After these six good games, the final contest was a travesty, with the Cards scoring seven times in the third inning and going on to win, 11-0. In the game, played in Detroit, Commissioner Landis was forced to remove Cardinal left fielder Joe 'Ducky' Medwick from action after an incredible display by vegetable-throwing loyal Tiger fans who were protesting his previous aggressive slide into third baseman Marv Owen. Dizzy Dean pitched a six-hitter to beat Auker – one of six pitchers used in the game by the Tigers. The Cardinals had triumphed, four games to three.

1935

Detroit Tigers 4, Chicago Cubs 2

Mickey Cochran's Tigers repeated their American League championship in 1935, after a struggle with the New York Yankees, finishing three games ahead of the pack. All during the National League season, it had been a fight between the New York Giants and the St Louis Cardinals, with the Giants leading most of the way. Then came September, and Charlie Grimm's Chicago Cubs came out of nowhere with a streak of 21 straight victories to win the pennant.

Buoyed up by their September momentum, the Cubs took the first game of the Series, 3-0, as Lon Warneke pitched a four-hitter to defeat Schoolboy Rowe. But the Bengals had no trouble with the Bruins in the second game, beating them 8-3, after handing winner Tommy Bridges a four-run lead in the first inning. Charlie Root was the loser. In the third game of the Series Detroit scored the winning run in the ninth inning. Rowe won this one, 6-5, beating Larry French. But Detroit suffered a potentially fatal loss in the game when first baseman Hank Greenberg, the Most Valuable Player in the American League that year, broke his wrist.

Still, Detroit increased its lead, three games to one, in the fourth game by winning 2-1 behind General Crowder, who threw a five-hitter to beat Charlie Root. Chicago came back in the fifth game with a 3-1 victory as Warneke beat Rowe once again. In this game, the Cubs' 'Arkansas Hummingbird' suffered a muscle injury, but Bill Lee came in to relieve, holding the Tigers to four hits in the final three innings.

Bridges faced French in the sixth game, and it was a close contest. Detroit scored in the first inning and Chicago tied it at 1-1 in the third. In the fourth, the Tigers scored another run, Chicago countered with two in the fifth, and the Bengals tied it again with one in the sixth. Going in the ninth, it was still deadlocked. Then Cub third baseman Stan Hack led off the inning with a triple. But Bridges took charge, striking out

LEFT: Cub Phil Cavarretta is out at first base in game two of the 1935 Series. The Cubs scored three runs to the Tigers' eight in this contest.

ABOVE: Sequence shots depict Cub pitcher Lon Warneke's motion in the 1935 Series opener. Warneke pitched a four-hit shutout, then later won game five on six shutout innings, coming out of the Series with a 0.54 ERA.

RIGHT: In the dressing room after driving in the winning run of the Series' sixth and final game, Tiger Goose Goslin is kissed by manager Mickey Cochrane (left) and pitcher Tommy Bridges.

shortstop Billy Jurges, tossing French out at first base, and retiring left fielder Augie Galan on an outfield fly. When the Tigers scored a run in the bottom of the ninth, they had won the game, 4-3, and the Series four games to two. Since the Tigers had lost their previous four Series and the Cubs had done the same, this contest between two World Series doormats had broken the jinx for Detroit.

1936

New York Yankees 4, New York Giants 2

The New York Giants took the National League pennant by five games in 1936, being built around the talents of the great pitcher Carl Hubbell. Hubbell was voted the Most Valuable Player in the league that year for his 26-6 record, closing the season with a winning streak of 16 games. In the American League there was no contest, the New York Yankees finishing 19 and a half games ahead of the Tigers. The fourth New York 'Subway Series' was about to begin.

The Giants, behind 'King Carl' Hubbell, had little trouble with the Yankees and Red Ruffing in the first game. The only run off Hubbell, who won his seventeenth straight game of the year, came in the third inning when right fielder George Selkirk homered. Giant shortstop Dick Bartell tied up the game with a home run in the fifth. The Giants went ahead for good in the sixth, when right fielder Mel Ott doubled and was driven home by catcher Gus Mancuso's single. Scoring four more runs in the eighth, the Giants won game one, 6-1.

But the Yanks stormed back in the second game, winning 18-4. In this game, Vernon 'Lefty' Gomez beat Giant starter Hal Schumacher. The game featured not only a seven-run third inning, but also a six-run ninth inning for the Bronx Bombers. The third game was a great deal closer, but the Yankees still managed to win, 2-1. Bump Hadley scattered 11 hits for the victory and Freddy Fitzsimmons, in a hard luck outing, gave up but four and still took the loss.

Hubbell was not invincible, however, and he lost the fourth game to the Yankees' Monte Pearson, 5-2. In the game, the Yanks were spurred on by their 'Iron Horse,' Lou Gehrig, who hit a two-run homer in the third inning. The Giants weren't down yet, and in the fifth contest they scored three runs in the first inning and one in the sixth, while the Yankees scored one run in the second and one in the third, adding another two to tie the score in the sixth. Then followed three scoreless innings. In the tenth, the Giants scored the winning

LEFT: Yankee Joe DiMaggio is safe at home in game six of the 1936 Series against the Giants. The Yankees won the game, 13-5, to take the Series four games to two. The Yankee Clipper batted .346 in his first Series appearance.

OPPOSITE TOP: Baseball commissioner Judge Landis (center) instructs the umpires in a meeting before the 1936 World Series. Left to right are Bill Summers and Harry Giesel, American League arbiters, and Cy Pfirman and George Magerkurth, National League umpires.

OPPOSITE BOTTOM: Yankee shortstop Frank Crosetti bobbles a Dick Bartell dribbler as Mel Ott charges home with the tying run in the sixth inning of game five. The Giants then took the game in the tenth on a Terry sacrifice fly.

run on a double by left fielder Jo-Jo Moore, a bunt by Bartell and a sacrifice fly by first baseman-manager Bill Terry.

After all these heroics, the sixth game was a disaster for the Giants. They started all right, scoring two runs in the first inning. But the Yankees tied the game in the second. At the end of eight innings, the Yankees led by a close score of 6-5. Then the roof fell in on the National Leaguers as the Yanks tallied seven times in the ninth on five hits and four walks to win the game, 13-5, and the World Series four games to two.

1937

New York Yankees 4, New York Giants 1

The Yankees repeated in 1937, winning 102 games for the second straight season and finishing 13 games ahead of Detroit to take the American League pennant. In the National League, the Giants had to come from behind in September to beat out the Cubs for the flag by three games. The stage was set for the fifth New York 'Subway Series.'

Carl Hubbell had had another splendid season for the Giants, but he was bombed out of the first game by the heavy-hitting Yankees. He lasted until the sixth inning when the Yankees erupted for seven runs. It seemed as if everyone had a hit, and the usually weak-hitting pitcher, Lefty Gomez, who became the winning hurler, got two walks in that big inning. It was not King Carl's day, and the game ended with the Yankees winning, 8-1.

Giant pitcher Cliff Melton had won 20 games in his rookie season, and he faced the Yankees in the second game. The result was another 8-1 game, with Red Ruffing getting the victory by scattering seven hits and aiding his own cause with two hits and three RBI's. The Yanks did it again in the third game, with Monte Pearson pitching a five-hitter and beating Hal Schumacher, 5-1.

The Giants finally won the fourth game behind Hubbell, who pitched a splendid six-hitter. The game seemed in the bag as early as the second inning, when the Giants took a 6-1 lead. They went on to win, 7-3, defeating Bump Hadley. The Yankees ended the Series in the fifth game by beating the Giants, 4-2 – with Gomez beating Melton. Although the Giants had 10 hits to the Yankees' eight, home runs by Joe DiMaggio and Myril Hoag helped win the game for the Yanks. The Series ended four games to one, and it had been a National League debacle. Of the Yankees' total of 42 hits, six were doubles, four were triples, and four were home runs.

LEFT: Yankee pitcher Red Ruffing (left) and Giant pitcher Cliff Melton shake hands at Yankee Stadium before the second game of the 1937 World Series. Melton was forced to retire when the Yanks got four hits and two runs off him in the fifth inning, while Ruffing supported his own pitching with two hits and three RBI's. The Yanks won it, 8-1.

RIGHT: Giant Joe Moore is out at first after hitting to Lou Gehrig, who flipped the ball to pitcher Lefty Gomez for the last play of the 1937 Series. The Yanks won the game, 4-2, and clinched the Series crown by taking four games to the Giants' one.

1938

New York Yankees 4, Chicago Cubs 0

Manager Joe McCarthy later called the 1938 Yankees the greatest team he ever fielded. The team won 99 games and finished nine and a half games ahead of the Boston Red Sox to take the American League pennant. The Chicago Cubs, on the other hand, were in a dogfight through the whole season, and ended with a mere 89 victories and a pathetic .586 winning average. When the Pirates came to Chicago for the last three games of the season, they were ahead by one and a half games. Dizzy Dean, just obtained from St Louis, beat them, 2-1, in the first game. In the next game, the score was tied going into the bottom of the ninth, and darkness was approaching, making it likely that the game would be declared a tie and be replayed as a part of a double-header the next day. But Cub catcher Gabby Hartnett, with two men out, came to bat. After two strikes, he connected with a fast ball from Mace Brown to win the game with his famous 'homer in the gloamin.' The Cubs were now a half game in front, and beat the dispirited Pirates, 10-1, the next day to take the championship.

Once again it was the Yankees against the Cubs. In the first game, Cub ace pitcher Bill Lee faced Red Ruffing. The Yankees scored two runs in the second inning and played a fine defensive game to beat Chicago, 3-1. Dean frightened New York for a time in the second game, as he held the Yankees to two runs on his nothing ball for seven innings, with the Cubs ahead 3-2. Then things fell apart. In the eighth inning, Yankee left fielder George Selkirk singled. After Myril Hoag batted for Gomez and forced Selkirk, shortstop Frankie Crosetti hit a home run. In the ninth, it was Joe DiMaggio who contributed a two-run homer, and Lefty Gomez had won his sixth World Series game, tying him with Chief Bender and Waite Hoyte.

It was all downhill for the Cubs after that. They lost 5-2 in the third game, in which Clay Bryant lost to Monte Pearson. The fourth game was worse. Chicago lost 8-3, with Ruffing once again beating Lee. Chalk up another Series sweep for the Yankees, who scored 22 runs to the Cubs' nine.

ABOVE: Cub Gabby Hartnett is surrounded by cheering teammates as he crosses the plate after hitting his 'homer in the gloamin' against the Pirates.

LEFT: The ball goes through Yankee second baseman Joe Gordon's legs as Cub Ken O'Dea slides in safely, in game four of the 1938 Series. The Yanks went on to win the game, 8-3.

RIGHT: The Cubs' newly acquired pitcher, Dizzy Dean, lost game two after pitching seven innings with a sore arm, and giving up only five hits.

1939

New York Yankees 4, Cincinnati Reds 0

Bill McKechnie's Cincinnati Reds took the National League pennant in 1939 – their first flag since 1919 – finishing four and a half games ahead of the Cardinals. Their championship was largely due to the pitching of Bucky Walters (27-11) and Paul Derringer (25-7). Again, the Yankees, who had been the first team to win three World Series in succession the year before, were the class of the American League, despite the resignation of the terminally ill first baseman Lou Gehrig. The Bronx Bombers ended the season with 106 wins and a 17-game lead over the Boston Red Sox.

The first game saw New York's Red Ruffing winning his fifth World Series game, 2-1, beating Paul Derringer. It was a thriller, with the winning run being scored in the bottom of the ninth inning. It was also a pitchers' duel, since the Yanks had but six hits and the Reds four. The second contest ended as a 4-0 triumph for the Yankees, with pitcher Monte Pearson being the star. He pitched no-hit ball until the eighth inning, when catcher Ernie Lombardi got a hit. Still, Pearson ended with a nifty two-hitter, beating Walters.

Lefty Gomez started the third game for the Yankees, but was forced to retire after the first inning because of a sore arm. Bump Hadley, in relief, got credit for his second Series win in this freak game. The Reds outhit the Yankees seven to five, but four of the five New York hits were home runs – two by right fielder Charlie 'King Kong' Keller, and one each by center fielder Joe DiMaggio and catcher Bill Dickey. The losing pitcher of this 7-3 game was Gene Thompson.

But the Reds had really not been humiliated. They had played good ball through three losing games, and had not made a single error. Indeed, they went through the first eight innings of the fourth game with no errors. With Cincinnati leading 4-2, New York tied it in the top of the ninth inning when shortstop Billy Myers booted a double-play ball. Then in the tenth, errors by Myers, right fielder Ival Goodman and Lombardi helped the Yankees to score three runs and win the game, 7-4, and the Series four games to none – their fourth straight world championship. This was the fifth time that the Bronx Bombers had won a World Series by sweeping all four games.

OPPOSITE TOP: Lou Gehrig, who retired after setting a record for consecutive games played, is honored at Yankee Stadium, 4 July 1939.

OPPOSITE BOTTOM: Yankees celebrate their 4-0 Series sweep over the Reds in the dressing room after game four.

ABOVE: Cincinnati's Ival Goodman strikes out on a Red Ruffing pitch at the end of the first inning of the 1939 Series opener. The Yanks won it in the ninth on an RBI single by Bill Dickey.

1940

Cincinnati Reds 4, Detroit Tigers 3

It was the last year before America would enter another world war, and the Cincinnati Reds repeated as National League champions, finishing in first place with a comfortable 12-game lead over the Brooklyn Dodgers. Both pitchers Bucky Walters and Paul Derringer had 20-game years – Walters winning 22 and Derringer taking 20. Bill McKechnie's star first baseman, powerhouse Frank McCormick, led the league in hits for the third straight year, and was voted Most Valuable Player in the National League. The only unfortunate occurrence during the season was the 3 August suicide of second-string catcher Willard Hershberger, who slashed his throat with a razor in the club's Boston hotel after several days of self-criticism for 'making a bad call.'

The Detroit Tigers surprised everybody by taking the American League pennant, clinching the championship on the next-to-last day of the season. Their winning percentage of .584 was the lowest of any American League champion up to that time, but they finished one game ahead of the Cleveland Indians and two games ahead of the New York Yankees.

Despite their mediocre record, the Bengals did win the first game of the Series. The score was 7-2, and Detroit's Bobo Newsom outpitched Derringer, who was removed in the Tigers' five-run second inning. (Newsom's father saw his son's triumph from the stands in Cincinnati's Crosley Field, but, tragically, he died of a heart attack the next day.) The Reds came back to take the second game, 5-3, on a magnificent three-hitter by Walters. He got off to a shaky start by walking the first two batters – both of whom scored. But the Reds then rapped Schoolboy Rowe for two runs in the second and scored two more in the third inning, going ahead on a two-run homer by left fielder Jimmy Ripple.

The third game started out as a pitching duel between Jim Turner of the Reds and Tommy Bridges of the Tigers, and the score was tied, 1-1, going into the seventh inning. Then first baseman Rudy York and third baseman Pinky Higgins of the Tigers hit home runs, and the Tigers went on to win the game, 7-4. Derringer came back in the fourth game. This time he scattered five hits, the Reds won, 5-2, and the Series was tied up once again. The losing pitcher was Paul 'Dizzy' Trout.

Newsom returned to pitch in the fifth game, and he turned in an impressive job, giving up but three hits. Left fielder Hank Greenberg led the 13-hit Tiger attack with a home run and two singles, driving in four runs to beat the Reds, 8-0. Cincinnati tied up the Series for the third time in the sixth game when Walters shut out the Tigers, 4-0, scattering five hits to beat Rowe for the second time.

After only one day's rest, Newsom was called on to pitch in the deciding seventh game, facing Derringer. It was a superb contest, and each pitcher allowed only seven hits. The Tigers tiptoed along on one unearned run until the seventh inning. Then, in the seventh, McCormick hit a double. Ripple followed this with another double, and Tiger shortstop Dick Bartell cut off the throw from the outfield that might have resulted in a putout at home plate. McCormick scored, then Ripple took third on an infield out and was driven home on a sacrifice fly by shortstop Billy Myers. The Reds won the game, 2-1, and the Series four games to three – their first championship since the tainted Series of 1919.

ABOVE: In the 1940 Series' seventh game, Cincinnati's pinch-runner Linus Frey dives safely back to first base as Detroit's Rudy York tries to tag him out.

LEFT: In game six the Reds' first baseman Frank McCormick drops the ball after fielding an Earl Averill hopper, beating the runner to the bag and crashing into the umpire. Averill was ruled safe on the play, but would not score to ruin Bucky Walters' shutout.

RIGHT: The Reds' Ernie Lombardi bangs a double in the second inning of game three, at Detroit's Briggs Stadium. The Reds were beaten, 7-4, on two Detroit homers in the seventh.

1941

New York Yankees 4, Brooklyn Dodgers 1

It was the New York Yankees again at the top of the heap in the American League in 1941, a season highlighted by Bronx Bomber center fielder Joe DiMaggio's record-breaking 56-game streak in which he had at least one hit in every contest. The Yanks clinched the pennant on 4 September and set a record for the earliest date ever in their one hundred thirty-sixth game.

In the National League the race was closer, with the Brooklyn Dodgers and the St Louis Cardinals in a dogfight all the way. The lead changed hands 27 times. The Cards led 11 times, the Dodgers seven, and the two teams were tied nine times. Under manager Leo Durocher the Dodgers finally captured the flag – their first in 21 years and the first time that the club had won 100 games in a season.

New York won the first game of this 'Subway Series,' 3-2. Red Ruffing joined Chief Bender, Waite Hoyte and Lefty Gomez in the six World Series victory class by scattering six hits to beat the Dodgers' ace Curt Davis. Second baseman Joe Gordon homered in the second inning. In the fourth, catcher Bill Dickey batted in another run with a double. The winning run came in the sixth on a walk and singles by Dickey and Gordon.

The Dodgers tied up the Series in the second contest by winning, 3-2. They got but six hits, but crowded four of them into the fifth and sixth innings. Whit Wyatt was the winning pitcher and Spud Chandler was the loser. The Yankees went ahead again in the third game, in which Marius Russo threw a four-hitter against Fred Fitzsimmons. Fitzsimmons also pitched quite a game, giving up only four hits in seven scoreless innings. He was hit on the knee by a line drive on the last out of the seventh and replaced in the eighth by Hugh Casey, who gave up singles to third baseman Red Rolfe, right fielder Tommy Henrich, DiMaggio and left fielder Charlie Keller that resulted in two Yankee runs. All that the Dodgers could do in the bottom of

OPPOSITE TOP: The would-be fourth-game-ending third strike gets away from Dodger catcher Mickey Owen as Tommy Henrich takes off to beat Owen's throw to first. The Yankees then snatched victory away with four runs, to take a commanding 3-1 Series lead.

RIGHT: Four sequence shots depict Yankee shortstop Phil Rizzuto turning a double play, with Cookie Lavagetto sliding in from first, in game three.

the eighth was to score once on a double by right fielder Dixie Walker and a single by shortstop Pee Wee Reese. The Yanks won, 2-1.

The fourth contest was close all the way. At the top of the ninth inning the Dodgers were ahead, 4-3, and apparently had the game in the bag when Henrich came to bat with two men out. Then disaster struck. Henrich swung at what was the third strike to end the game, but catcher Mickey Owen dropped the ball and Henrich made it to first base. The Yankees went on to stage a rally, scoring four runs on a single by DiMaggio, a double by Keller, a walk to Dickey and a double by Gordon, winning the game 7-4. Johnny Murphy was the winning pitcher and Casey was the loser – both in relief.

Ernie Bonham gave up only four hits to the Dodgers – and only one hit after the third inning – in the fifth game, as he faced Wyatt, who gave up a mere six hits himself. In the second inning, the Yankees scored all the runs that they needed on a walk, a single by Dickey, a wild pitch and another single by Gordon. Wyatt did all he could at the plate in the third inning. He doubled and the hit was followed by a single by third baseman Lew Riggs. Center fielder Pete Reiser's sacrifice fly scored Wyatt with the Dodgers' only run. The final Yankee run came on a homer by Henrich in the fifth inning. The Yankees had won the game, 3-1, and their ninth World Series, four games to one.

1942

St Louis Cardinals 4, New York Yankees 1

The year of 1942 saw the St Louis Cardinals back in the World Series. Billy Southworth's men had taken the National League championship on a great stretch drive. They had trailed the Brooklyn Dodgers by 10 and a half games as late as mid-August, but ended up two games in front at the end of the season, although second-place Brooklyn had won 104 games – usually enough to win a pennant. In the American League, the Yankees, as usual, won the flag – their sixth in seven years.

The United States had entered World War II in December of the preceding year, so 1942 was the first baseball season during that war. As was true in World War I, there were many who felt that the games should be cancelled. But President Franklin D Roosevelt, shortly after the declaration of war, wrote to Baseball Commissioner Kenesaw Mountain Landis, 'I honestly feel that it would be best for the country to keep baseball going.' And baseball kept going, although more than 300 major-league players would go into service in the next two years, and those who stayed behind had legitimate exemptions.

In the first game of the World Series, Red Ruffing held the Cardinals hitless until the eighth inning, at which point the Yankees were ahead by a score of 5-0. With two out in the eighth, center fielder Terry Moore of the Cards singled but did not score. The Yanks scored two more runs in the top of the ninth. But in the bottom of that inning the youthful, inexperienced Cardinals found themselves. With two outs, the Cardinals began to threaten with a series of walks and hits. Before reliever Spud Chandler could pitch the final out, the Cards had scored four runs. The game ended 7-4 with Ruffing the winner – becoming the first pitcher to win seven World Series games – and Mort Cooper the loser.

St Louis came back to tie the Series in the second game. Cardinals Enos Slaughter and Stan Musial were the heroes of this one, when they came to bat in the bottom of the eighth inning with the score tied, 3-3. A double and a single scored what turned out to to be the winning run when great Cardinal defense held the Yanks from scoring in the ninth, and rookie pitcher Johnny Beazley got the win over Ernie Bonham, 4-3. Everybody assumed that the Yankee bats would come alive in the third game – which they did – but Cardinal outfielders Moore, Musial and Slaughter took turns making spectacular catches. The game ended with the Cards winning 2-0 on a six-hitter by Ernie White. Spud Chandler, who allowed only five hits, was the loser in this shutout – the Yankees' first scoreless World Series game since they were blanked by Cardinal Jesse Haines in 1926.

Game four seesawed back and forth, first 1-0 Yankees, then 6-1 Cardinals, then 6-6 after six innings. The roof fell in the seventh, when the Cards scored two runs, and in the ninth they got another. The winning pitcher in this 9-6 game was Max Lanier and the loser was Atley Donald – both of them in relief.

Ruffing faced Beazley in the fifth game, and it was a close one. New York scored one run in the first inning, and held that lead until the fourth, when St Louis scored a run. But the Bombers went ahead by one run in the bottom of the fourth. The Cardinals tied the game, 2-2, in the sixth. Then came the fateful ninth inning. Rookie third baseman Whitey Kurowski was the hero when he hit a two-run homer in the top of the inning. The final Yankee indignity was suffered by second baseman Joe Gor-

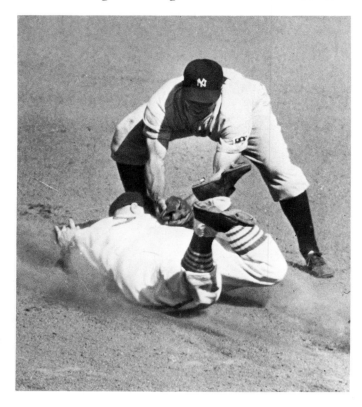

don of the Yankees. Although he had been elected Most Valuable Player in the American League for the season, he hit only .095 in the Series, and in that ninth inning he let Card catcher Walker Cooper pick him off second base, wiping out New York's final threat. The Cardinals had won the World Series, four games to one.

ABOVE: Heavy-hitting Cardinals and Yankees pose before the 1942 World Series opener. Left to right are Joe DiMaggio, Enos Slaughter, Charlie Keller and Terry Moore. In game one Keller went hitless, but the other three accounted for six of the 18-hit total.

LEFT: Jimmy Brown of the Cards slides safely into second base during game two. Brown's .300 batting average was the highest of his regular lineup teammates' during the Series.

RIGHT: National League president Ford Frick (left) and St Louis Cardinal Vice President Branch Rickey (right) congratulate Cardinal manager Billy Southworth, as he is held aloft by jubilant players, after the Cards won the 1942 World Series.

1943

New York Yankees 4, St Louis Cardinals 1

Because of the war, professional baseball seemed to be on hold, so it was no surprise that in 1943 both the Yankees and the Cardinals won their league titles once again. The Yankees finished the season with 98 wins and a lead of 13 and a half games over the Washington Senators. In the National League, the Cardinals won 105 games and outdistanced the second-place Cincinnati Reds by 18 games.

The Yankees, as they had the year before, won the first game. It was a seesaw battle for a while, but the Yanks scored two runs on an error and a wild pitch by Max Lanier to win it, 4-2. The winner was Spud Chandler and the loser was Lanier. St Louis gave their fans some hope in the second game. But once again tragedy had struck during the World Series. The starting Cardinal battery for this game consisted of pitcher Mort Cooper and his brother, catcher Walker Cooper, who played the game despite the death of their father that morning. Cooper beat the Bronx Bombers and pitcher Ernie Bonham, 4-3, on home runs by shortstop Marty Marion and first baseman Ray Sanders.

Alpha Brazle of the Cards faced Hank Borowy of the Yanks in the third game, and it was a pitchers' duel until the eighth inning. When New York came to bat in the bottom of that inning, St Louis was leading, 2-1. Right fielder Johnny Lindell was the first man up and he singled, advancing to second on center fielder Harry Walker's error in retrieving the ball. George 'Snuffy' Stirnweiss came in to pinch-hit for Borowy and laid down a bunt toward first base. The first baseman, Ray Sanders, grabbed the ball and threw to third baseman Whitey Kurowski. Lindell appeared out by several steps, but he crashed into Kurowski, knocking the ball from his hand, and both runners were safe. After center fielder Tuck Stainback flied out, Lindell was still on third but Stirnweiss had taken second. Shortstop Frankie Crosetti was walked intentionally, filling the

LEFT: Yankee hurler Spud Chandler demonstrates his follow-through. Chandler posted two wins in the '43 Series, including the fifth and deciding game shutout.

OPPOSITE TOP: British Broadcasting Company announcer Don Dunphy calls the Series opener play-by-play for soldiers in England, Africa and Italy.

OPPOSITE BOTTOM: In the eighth inning of game three, Yankee baserunner John Liddell successfully implores the umpire to let him remain on third base, after Liddell slid and Cardinal third baseman dropped the ball. The Yanks scored five runs this inning for a 6-2 victory.

bases. Then third baseman Billy Johnson cleared the bases with a triple. A walk and three more hits gave the Yanks two more runs for a 6-2 victory.

That seemed to take the spirit out of Billy Southworth's club, since they were able to score only one run in the last two games. They lost the fourth game, 2-1, with Marius Russo the winner and Harry Brecheen the loser, and were shut out in the fifth contest by Spud Chandler, who beat Mort Cooper, 2-0. The Cardinal hitters stranded 11 men. The Yanks took the Series by the same four games to one as in the previous year, but with a switch in roles for the two teams. This gave the Yankees their tenth world championship and their seventh under manager Joe McCarthy. It was to be the last for McCarthy, who left in 1946.

1944

St Louis Cardinals 4, St Louis Browns 2

The year 1944 gave baseball fans a contest that will never be repeated – an all-St Louis Series. As far as the available talent was concerned, this year was probably the nadir for major-league baseball. In the American League, the Detroit Tigers and the New York Yankees were in a pennant battle, with the St Louis Browns nipping at their heels. The Browns had not won a pennant in the twentieth century, but managed by Luke Sewell, they managed to take the flag by one game, sweeping the Yankees in the final four-game series of the year. The Browns' stars were veteran hitters Mike Kreevich and Vern Stephens, and their pitching aces were Jack Kramer and Nelson Potter.

In the National League, Billy Southworth's Cardinals won their third consecutive championship behind the pitching of Mort Cooper, with his 22 wins; Ted Wilks (released by the Army with a stomach ulcer), with 17; and George Munger, who had an 11-3 record before joining the service in July. Thus the 'trolley series' began, and it was to be a Series of superb pitching by both clubs and inept fielding by the Browns.

In the first game, Mort Cooper was in a pitching duel with the Browns' Denny Galehouse. But Cooper, who gave up only two hits in the entire game, gave up a single to right fielder Gene Moore in the fourth inning, and this was followed by first baseman George McQuinn's home run. The Cardinals tried a come-back in the ninth, scoring one run, but the game went to the Browns, 2-1. The second game went into extra innings with the score tied, 2-2, at the end of nine. Then, in the bottom of the eleventh, Cardinal first base-man Ray Sanders singled; this was followed by a sacrifice bunt and a single by pinch-hitter Ken O'Dea. The Cardinals had won, 3-2, with the winning pitcher reliever Sylvester Donnelly and the loser Bob Muncrief, also in relief.

The Browns surprised everyone by coming back to win the third game. In this one, they routed Cardinal

starter Wilks with four runs in the third inning to give Kramer a 6-2 win. Then the Cards came back to sweep the final three games. In the fourth game, Cardinal pitcher Harry Brecheen beat Sid Jakucki, 5-1 – the big blow in the game being right fielder Stan Musial's two-run homer. Cooper came back to defeat Denny Galehouse, 2-0, in the fifth game on home runs by Sanders and left fielder Danny Litwhiler. The sixth game was really won in the fourth inning when the Cards scored three runs for pitcher Max Lanier for a 3-1 victory. Cardinal reliever Wilks retired the last 11 Browns' batters to help defeat Nelson Potter, and the Cardinals had won the Series four games to two. But the key had been the fielding. The Cardinals had committed but one error to the Browns' ten.

LEFT: 'Doc' Weaver hugs Cardinal pitcher Harry Brecheen after he hurled his club to a 5-1 game four victory in the 1914 Series. 'The Cat' had posted a 16-5 record during the regular season.

OPPOSITE TOP: Cardinal pitcher Max Lanier is safe at first on a wide throw from Brown pitcher Nelson Potter, in the 1944 Series' second game. The Cards eked out a win in the eleventh inning, 3-2.

OPPOSITE BOTTOM: Cardinal Whitey Kurowski scores in the fourth inning of the Series' sixth and final game. The Cards went on to take the game, 3-1, and become World Series champions.

1945

Detroit Tigers 4, Chicago Cubs 3

In 1945 the Chicago Cubs, spearheaded by first baseman Phil Cavarretta and ace pitcher Hank Borowy, edged out the St Louis Cardinals, winning the flag on the next-to-last day of the season. Cavarretta hit .355 that season to win the National League's Most Valuable Player Award, and Borowy came to Charlie Grimm's Cubs from the Yankees in July, promptly going 11-2 for the Bruins. Those 11 wins, plus what he had already won for New York, made him the only pitcher in history to have a 20-game season while pitching in both leagues.

The Detroit Tigers also had to fight for their pennant, beating out the Washington Senators on the last day of the season when Hank Greenberg, who had been let out of the Air Force in Europe, beat the St Louis Browns on a grand slam home run. Ace pitcher Virgil Trucks was back from the Navy, and the Tigers also had lefthander Hal Newhouser in their pitching rotation, plus the slugging Rudy York at first base. It was to become one of the most thrilling World Series of all time.

In the first game, Borowy posted a shutout over Newhouser, who was relieved in the third inning by the second of four pitchers. The Cubs, after scoring four runs in the top of the first inning, went on to win, 9-0, with Borowy scattering six hits. In the second game, Trucks, out of the service for less than a week, beat Hank Wyse, 4-1, on a three-run home run by Greenberg in the fifth inning.

Claude Passeau of the Cubs pitched a masterpiece in the third game. It was a one-hitter, the only blow being a single by Rudy York in the second inning. Passeau walked but one man, and since both Tiger runners were erased in double plays, he faced only 27 men in what was the greatest World Series pitching feat up to that time. The Cubs won, 3-0, and the loser was Stubby Overmire. Then, in the fourth game, it was Detroit's turn again. Dizzy Trout threw a five-hitter at the Cubs, beating Ray Prim, 4-1.

LEFT: Cubs (left to right) Phil Cavarretta, Hank Borowy, Andy Pafko and Bill Nicholson celebrate their 9-0 victory over Detroit in the '45 Series opener.

ABOVE: Tiger Hank Greenberg trots around the bases after unleashing a three-run homer in the fifth inning of game two.

BELOW: Tiger pitcher Hal Newhouser is embraced in the dressing room after pitching his team to a 9-3 seventh-game victory.

In game five Newhouser struck out nine Cubs and Greenberg laced three doubles for an 8-4 victory over Borowy. Chicago came back to tie the Series in the sixth game. This one was a box score nightmare. Nineteen players were used by each team. After five innings, the Cubs were ahead by a comfortable 4-1 score, but in the sixth Detroit third baseman Jimmy Outlaw hit a hard smash to the mound that ripped the nail off the middle finger of the right hand of the pitcher – Passeau – who had to leave the game in the seventh. Detroit scored four runs in the eighth, tying the game 7-7. The Cubs finally scored in the twelfth to win, 8-7, with Borowy, in relief, the winner.

The final game was a disaster for the Cubs – beginning when the Bengals scored five runs in the top of the first. Borowy, who had appeared in the previous two games, was simply too tired. He failed to retire a single batter, giving up a quick run on successive singles by shortstop Skeeter Webb, second baseman Eddie Mayo and center fielder Roger Kramer. The horrible inning continued with Paul Derringer in relief. Greenberg sacrificed and right fielder Roy Cullenbine was intentionally walked. Third baseman Jimmy Outlaw was unintentionally walked, which forced in a run. Then catcher Paul Richards cleaned the bases with a double, and the Tigers kept their lead until the end. Newhouser won the game, 9-3, and the Tigers the Series.

1946

St Louis Cardinals 4, Boston Red Sox 3

Ted Williams carried the Boston Red Sox to the American League title in 1946. He had just returned from service, and promptly hit .342, with 38 homers and 123 RBI's, leading the Sox to their first pennant since 1918. Of course he had plenty of help in the hitting department from shortstop Johnny Pesky, center fielder Dom DiMaggio, first baseman Rudy York and second baseman Bobby Doerr. The Sox won by 12 games over the Detroit Tigers.

In the National League, Eddie Dyer's St Louis Cardinals had a rough time. They ended the season in a first-place tie with the Brooklyn Dodgers, necessitating the first pennant playoff in major-league history. The Cards took two straight games of the best two out of three series, and captured the flag.

The Redbirds had been in eight World Series up to this time, and had lost the first game in seven of them. This year game one found them ahead, 2-1, going into the ninth inning, and with Howie Pollet on the mound. But a grounder by Boston third baseman Pinky Higgins took a freak hop and the Sox tied the score. York hit a homer in the tenth to win the game for Boston and relief pitcher Earl Johnson, 3-2.

St Louis came back in the second game, winning 3-0 on a four-hitter by Harry Brecheen. The loser was Mickey Harris. Then it was Boston's turn in the third game. And it was the second straight shutout in the Series. This time the pitcher was Dave 'Boo' Ferriss, who scattered six hits in the 4-0 game, with Murry Dickson taking the loss. The Cards won the fourth game to tie the Series behind the pitching of George Munger. St Louis got 20 hits in the contest for a final tally of 12-3, with Cecil Hughson taking the loss.

The seesaw series continued, as Boston won the fifth game, when Joe Dobson defeated Alpha Brazle, 6-3, on a four-hitter. The Cardinals' backs were against the wall, and they once again called on Harry Brecheen to save the day in the sixth game. Once again Harris was his opponent. Brecheen – 'The Cat' – scattered seven

ABOVE: Cardinal Enos Slaughter slides home safely with the Series-winning run in the eighth inning of game seven. Red Sox catcher Roy Partee waits in vain for the throw from shortstop Johnny Pesky.

hits as the Cards tied up the Series, 6-3.

The finale pitted Dickson against Ferriss. The Redbirds got to Ferriss and held a 3-1 lead going into the eighth inning. Boston manager Joe Cronin called on two straight pinch-hitters, and they both delivered, when Glen Russell singled and was advanced to third on a double by George Metkovich. Brecheen came in to relieve and retired the first two batters, but then a double by Dom DiMaggio tied the score. Then in the bottom of the eighth Cardinal right fielder Enos 'Country' Slaughter singled off reliever Bob Klinger. After two outs, catcher Harry Walker singled and Slaughter raced home from first with the winning run, as shortstop Johnny Pesky hesitated with the throw. The Cardinals had won the game, 4-3, and the Series four games to three.

OPPOSITE: The Cardinal defense shifts right as Boston's Splendid Splinter, Ted Williams, comes to the plate in the Series opener.

ABOVE: Pitchers Dave Ferriss (left) and Murry Dickson shake hands. Both threw in game three and game seven.

95

1947

New York Yankees 4, Brooklyn Dodgers 3

The 1947 World Series was memorable – mostly because it was the first Series in which a black man participated – the immortal first baseman Jackie Robinson. During the regular season Burt Shotten's Brooklyn Dodgers, a team that featured this future Hall of Famer, had a close battle with the St Louis Cardinals. The New York Yankees, under manager Bucky Harris, who won his second pennant as a freshman manager (the other being at the helm of the Washington Senators in 1924), breezed into the championship with a 12-game lead over the Detroit Tigers in the American League.

The first game was a big disappointment for Brooklyn. Their pitching ace, Ralph Branca, retired the first 12 Yankees who faced him. With the score tied 0-0 in the fifth, the Yankees exploded for five runs and went on to take the game, 5-3, behind the pitching of Spec Shea. The Yankees also won the second game, 10-3, as Yankee pitcher Allie Reynolds scattered nine hits and struck out 10 to beat Vic Lombardi. Brooklyn finally won a game, the third contest, when they beat Bobo Newsom, their former teammate, 9-8. The winner was Hugh Casey.

The fourth game was a barnburner. Bill Bevens, the Yankee starting pitcher, had had a pathetic record that year, winning only seven games and losing 13. But he held the Dodgers hitless for eight and two-thirds innings. He was wild – walking 10 men – and that led to a Brooklyn run in the fifth inning on two walks, a sacrifice bunt and an infield out. The roof fell in in the ninth inning. With one out, Brooklyn center fielder Carl Furillo walked, and this was followed by third baseman Johnny Jorgensen's foul-out. Al Gionfriddo, sent in to run for Furillo, stole second. Dodger Pete Reiser stepped up to pinch–hit for pitcher Casey, and Harris ordered Bevens to walk him. Eddie Miksis came in to run for Reiser, and Cookie Lavagetto was sent up to bat for second baseman Eddie Stanky. Then came another shot heard round the world, when Lavagetto crashed a double off the right field wall to score two runs. Bevens still had a one-hitter, but Brooklyn had the ballgame, 3-2. Hugh Casey, in relief, was the winner.

Spec Shea was back on the mound for the Yankees in the fifth game, and threw a fine four-hitter to beat Rex Barney, 2-1. The Dodgers tied up the Series for the second time in the sixth game, which was a wild one indeed. The final score was 8-6, Brooklyn, with 38 players making an appearance in the game. This time the hero was the rookie Al Gionfriddo, who went into the game as a defensive switch to play left field in the sixth inning, with the Dodgers ahead, 8-5. Later in the inning, two Yankees were on base when Joe DiMaggio hit an apparent home run to left field. Gionfriddo raced to the left field bullpen and pulled down this 415-foot drive in a spectacular catch. Branca was the winner and reliever Joe Page was the loser.

The final game was a close one for a while. Shea was back on the mound for the Yankees, but he was knocked out in the second inning when the Dodgers scored two runs. Brooklyn pitcher Hal Gregg gave up a run in the bottom of the second, and was knocked out in the fourth when the Yanks scored two more. Reliever Joe Page threw the last five innings for the Yankees, and was the winner in this 5-2 contest. Gregg was the loser. The Yanks had taken yet another world championship, four games to three.

ABOVE: Dodger manager Burt Shotten hugs outfielder Al Gionfriddo after game six, which the Dodgers won on Gionfriddo's spectacular catch of a Joe DiMaggio line shot, evening the Series at three games each.

OPPOSITE TOP: Yankee Floyd Bevens pitching in game four, which he lost on one hit in the bottom of the ninth.

OPPOSITE BOTTOM: Dodger Cookie Lavagetto pinch-hits the game-winning double in the ninth inning of game four.

1948

Cleveland Indians 4, Boston Braves 2

The Boston Braves, a pretty pedestrian club, won the National League flag in 1948. Actually, about all that manager Billy Southworth had going for him were his two star pitchers, Warren Spahn, with 24 wins, and Johnny Sain, with 15, leading to the bit of doggerel, 'Spahn and Sain and pray for rain.' Still, Boston had little trouble in the pennant race, and this was their first pennant in 34 years.

In the American League, Lou Boudreau's Cleveland Indians were in third place, four and a half games out after Labor Day. Then they turned around and made a stretch drive to land in first place. But on the last day of the season, they lost to the Detroit Tigers as the Red Sox beat the Yankees. A one-game playoff was held, and Cleveland beat the Red Sox, 8-3, on the strength of player-manager Boudreau's two homers.

In the first game of the Series, Navy veteran and long-time star pitcher for the Indians, Bob Feller, made his first World Series start, facing Sain. The game was a heartbreaker for him. He allowed only two hits. In the eighth inning, Braves' catcher Bill Salkeld walked and Phil Masi was sent in to run for him. Center fielder Mike McCormick sacrificed Masi to second and second baseman Eddie Stanky was walked intentionally. Feller whirled and threw to shortstop Boudreau, who was trying a pickoff play. It was a disputed call, but Masi was safe. When right fielder Tommy Holmes singled, the Indians had lost, 1-0.

Cleveland came back in the next game, however, with Bob Lemon beating Spahn, 4-1. In the third game, war hero Gene Bearden beat Vern Bickford for another Cleveland victory, 2-0, in a five-hitter. The fourth game was another Indian win, with Steve Gromek defeating Sain, 2-1, with the help of a 410-foot home run by center fielder Larry Doby – the first black player in the American League.

Up to this point it had been a pitchers' Series, but in the fifth game the Braves exploded. Feller started the

game, but was driven out by a six-run rally in the seventh inning. Boston won the game, 11-5, with Spahn the winner and Feller the loser. In the sixth game Indian starter Bob Lemon was coasting along with a 4-1 lead until the eighth inning, when the Braves loaded the bases with only one out. Bearden relieved, but the Braves scored two runs before coming up short. Bill Voiselle was the loser as the Indians won the game, 4-3, and the Series, four games to two.

LEFT: The Braves' Sibby Sisti pops out while attempting to bunt in the ninth inning of game six. Catcher Jim Hegan threw to first to double up Connie Ryan and snuff the potential Boston rally. The Indians went on to take the game, 4-3, and the Series, four games to two.

OPPOSITE: Cleveland's Bob Feller and Boston's Johnny Sain, starting pitchers in the 1948 Series opener, shake hands before the game. Feller allowed only two hits in the game, but lost, 1-0.

BELOW: Brave pinch-runner Phil Masi is safe at second on an attempted pick-off play when Feller threw to Lou Boudreau in the eighth inning of game one. The play proved crucial as Masi was singled home by Tommy Holmes moments later with the game-winning run.

1949

New York Yankees 4, Brooklyn Dodgers 1

Casey Stengel's New York Yankees took the American League pennant on the last day of the season. They had been one game behind the powerful Boston Red Sox going into their final two-game series with the Sox, but won both of the games to finish one game ahead. In the National League the Brooklyn Dodgers were ahead of the league by one game going into the final day, but were forced to go into extra innings to beat the Philadelphia Phillies in the tenth, thus coming in ahead of the St Louis Cardinals.

The Series started off as a pitchers' duel. In the first game, Allie Reynolds of the Yankees was pitted against Don Newcombe of the Dodgers. Reynolds blanked the Dodgers on a mere two hits, and Newcombe had given up but four until the ninth inning, when first baseman Tommy Henrich hit a home run to give the New Yorkers a 1-0 victory. In the next game, the Dodgers' Preacher Rowe returned the compliment. Facing Vic Raschi, Rowe hung in there for yet another 1-0 game, with the Dodgers winning on a double by second baseman Jackie Robinson, followed by a single by first baseman Gil Hodges in the second inning.

The third game started out as another pitchers' battle, with Tommy Byrne pitching for the Yankees and Ralph Branca pitching for the Dodgers. In the third inning, the Yankees scored a run on a walk, a single by Byrne and a sacrifice fly by shortstop Phil Rizzuto. Dodger shortstop Pee Wee Reese tied the game with a home run in the fourth. Page came in to relieve Byrne and things went along scorelessly until the ninth inning. In the top of the inning, Yankee catcher Yogi Berra walked with one out. Center fielder Joe DiMaggio then fouled out, but third baseman Bobby Brown singled and left fielder Gene Woodling walked to fill the bases. Johnny Mize then batted for right fielder Cliff Mapes and singled, driving in two runs. Jack Banta relieved for Branca, but second baseman Jerry Coleman's single drove in a third run. This hit was the game-winner, because although Dodger left fielder Luis Olmo and catcher Roy Campanella both hit home runs in the bottom of the ninth, Page struck out pinch-hitter Bruce Edwards to end the game, saving a 4-3 Yankee win.

The excitement of the Series was over. In the fourth game, Newcomb and Eddie Lopat were the rival pitchers, but Newk fell apart in the fourth inning (he had had but two days rest), and gave up three runs on a walk and doubles by Brown, Mapes and Lopat. Joe Hatten came in to relieve and gave up three more runs. Lopat did bog down in the sixth, when the Dodgers scored four runs, but Reynolds came in to put out the fire. The Yanks won the game, 6-4.

Six Dodger pitchers couldn't prevent the Yankees from winning the fifth game, 10-6, and the Series, four games to one.

LEFT: Yankee ace Allie Reynolds pitching a two-hit shutout to beat the Dodgers, 1-0, in the 1949 Series opener.

OPPOSITE TOP: Dodger Jackie Robinson runs home to score for Brooklyn, giving his team their first run of the Series in the second inning of the second game. Dodger Gil Hodges heads for first on his single to left.

OPPOSITE BOTTOM: Yankee Phil 'Scooter' Rizzuto singles in the first inning of game four, at Ebbets Field, as Brooklyn's pitcher Don Newcombe watches the ball in flight.

1950

New York Yankees 4, Philadelphia Phillies 0

The closing out of the 1950 season found the New York Yankees struggling for the American League pennant. The Yanks had brought up rookie pitcher Whitey Ford in June from their Kansas City American Association club, and he had won nine straight games for them during the season to help the Bronx Bombers finish three games ahead of the Detroit Tigers. The 1950 National League flag went to the Philadelphia Phillies. Nicknamed 'The Whiz Kids' for their spirited play and their youth – their average age was only 26 – they had had a real battle with the Brooklyn Dodgers. The Phillies won the championship on the last day of the season by beating the Dodgers, 4-1, a victory that featured a home run by left fielder Dick Sisler.

The Philadelphia star pitcher was Robin Roberts, who was the first Philly to win 20 games since 1917. But since he had pitched in three of the final five games during the season, manager Eddie Sawyer chose to go with Jim Konstanty in the opening game of the Series. Konstanty that year had been the best pitcher in the bullpen, winning 16 games in 74 relief appearances, and being the first reliever ever to be named the National League's Most Valuable Player. He and Vic Raschi engaged in a tremendous mound duel in the game, Raschi giving up only two hits and Konstanty but four in eight innings. But the difference was a double in the fourth inning by Yankee third baseman Bobby Brown, that was followed by two sacrifice flies. The game went to the Yankees, 1-0.

Roberts opposed Allie Reynolds in the second game, and again it was a pitchers' duel, with the score standing at 1-1 going into extra innings. But in the tenth inning, center fielder Joe DiMaggio hit a home run, and the Yanks took the game, 2-1.

Ken Heintzelman started the third game for the Phillies, facing Eddie Lopat. In the seventh inning the

LEFT: Yankee Bobby Brown scores the only run of the 1950 Series opener at Shibe Park. Brown scored from third on Gerry Coleman's long fly in the fourth inning, in support of Vic Raschi's two-hitter.

OPPOSITE: Sequence shots depict eighth-inning action in the Series' second game, as the Phillies' speedy Rickie Ashburn is thrown out at second by pitcher Allie Reynolds, who fielded the Dick Sisler bunt and threw to Phil Rizzuto. The score remained tied, 1-1, until a tenth-inning DiMaggio homer won it for the Yankees.

Phils scored a run to go ahead, 2-1. It was still 2-1 in the eighth when, with two men out, Heintzelman seemed to lose control, walking three straight batters to load the bases. Konstanty came in to relieve and forced Brown to hit a grounder to shortstop Granny Hamner, who muffed the play and let in a run. In the ninth, the Yankees came to bat with the score tied. Left fielder Gene Woodling hit a grounder to second baseman Jimmy Bloodworth, who fumbled the ball. Shortstop Phil Rizzuto then hit a stinging line drive to Bloodworth, who couldn't hold the ball, and second baseman Jerry Coleman singled, scoring Woodling for a 3-2 victory. The winner was Tom Ferrick and the loser was Russ Meyer, both in relief.

The Phillies really were never a threat in the fourth game. In the first inning, the Yankees knocked out rookie Bob Miller, scoring two runs.

ABOVE: Philly second baseman Jimmy Bloodworth loses the ball after making a sensational stop of a Phil Rizzuto grounder in the ninth inning of the 1950 Series' game three. Rizzuto is safe and the infield hit set the stage for Gerry Coleman's game-winning single moments later.

OPPOSITE: The Yankees' Ed Ford held the Phillies to seven hits in the Series' fourth and final game. Allie Reynolds registered the save in the ninth inning, for a 5-2 New York victory.

They got three more in the sixth, one of them being on a home run by rookie catcher Yogi Berra. The Phils couldn't mount any offense until the ninth, when Woodling made an error on catcher Andy Seminick's fly ball, thus allowing two runs to score. The final score was 5-2, the winner was Whitey Ford, and the loser was Miller. The Yanks had taken yet another Series with a sweep, four games to none.

1951

New York Yankees 4, New York Giants 2

The New York Giants under Leo Durocher made the most historic run toward the pennant since the Miracle Braves of 1914. Starting on 12 August, the Giants won 16 consecutive games (with the Dodgers losing nine out of 18). By 9 September they were only five and a half games behind Brooklyn. Then the Giants won 16 of their last 20 (while the Dodgers lost 11) to force the pennant race into a playoff. Jim Hearn took the opening game of the best two out of three series, the Giants beating the Dodgers, 3-1. Behind pitcher Clem Labine, the Dodgers came back to beat the Giants, 10-0, in the second game. The Dodgers were leading the deciding game, 4-1, when in the bottom of the ninth, Giant shortstop Alvin Dark singled, Don Mueller singled and left fielder Monte Irvin popped out. Then first baseman Whitey Lockman doubled, driving Dark home and putting the tying runs on second and third. Pitcher Ralph Branca relieved Don Newcombe to face third baseman Bobby Thomson. After taking one strike, he drove the ball into the left field stands – 'the home run heard round the world' – and the Giants had the pennant.

In the American League, Casey Stengel's Yankees, as usual, won the flag, but not until they had beat off the Cleveland Indians. The Bombers finished five games in front.

In the first game of the Series, Durocher made a surprise move by starting Dave Koslo, although the southpaw had had a mediocre 10-9 year. But Koslo came through to defeat Allie Reynolds, 5-1, with left fielder Monte Irvin getting four hits and stealing home – the first theft of home plate in a World Series since 1928. Shortstop Alvin Dark clinched the victory with a three-run homer in the sixth.

In the second game, Eddie Lopat beat the Giants, 3-1, throwing a five-hitter, with Larry Jansen being the loser. The Giants came back in the third game, 6-2, with Jim Hearn defeating Vic Raschi. The highlight of the contest was a play by second baseman Eddie Stanky. The Giants were leading, 1-0, in the fifth inning. With one out, Raschi walked Stanky. With Dark at the plate, the Giants were prepared for a hit-and-run play, but catcher Yogi Berra called for a pitch-out and threw to shortstop Phil Rizzuto. Rizzuto had the ball and was waiting for Stanky to slide into second base. Stanky, however, kicked the ball out of Rizzuto's hand, got up, and ran to third. Dark singled him home, and the Giants proceeded to score four more runs in the inning.

BELOW: A historic photo of 'the home run heard round the world' depicts Giant Bobby Thomson's pennant-winning ninth-inning homer against the the Dodgers in the third playoff game in 1951.

OPPOSITE TOP: In a key play in game three, Giant Eddie Stanky slides into second on a steal, kicking the ball from Phil Rizzuto's glove and sparking the Giants' five-run rally.

OPPOSITE BOTTOM: Yankee rookie Gil McDougald belts a grand slam in game five.

Then the rains came, and that might have been the cause of the downfall of the Giants. With two days of showers, Reynolds was ready to pitch again, and beat the Giants in the fourth game, 6-2, the losing pitcher being Sal Maglie. Rookie third baseman Gil McDougald broke up the fifth game in the third inning with a grand slam home run – only the third time that feat had been accomplished in a World Series. In this game, Lopat beat Jansen, 13-1.

The sixth game was a hard-fought one. Koslo was facing Raschi, and going into the Yankee half of the sixth inning, the score was tied, 1-1. Then right fielder Hank Bauer hit a bases-loaded triple to drive in three runs. The Giants battled back in the ninth. Stanky singled and Dark bunted safely. When first baseman Lockman singled, the bases were full with no one out. Bob Kuzava came in to relieve Johnny Sain, who had replaced Raschi. Monte Irvin hit a long sacrifice fly that scored Stanky and allowed the other runners to advance. Another sacrifice fly, this time by Thomson, scored another run, making the score 4-3. But that was it. Pinch-hitter Sal Yvars sliced a low line drive to right field and Bauer made a spectacular running catch of the ball. The Yanks had taken another World Series, this time four games to two.

1952

New York Yankees 4, Brooklyn Dodgers 3

The Dodgers came back strong to take the National League flag in 1952. Actually, the Giants took the league lead early in the year, but when center fielder Willie Mays was inducted into the Army on 29 May, they lost eight of their next 10 games and never recovered. As usual, it was the Yankees in the American League.

Dodger manager Charlie Dressen chose Joe Black to oppose Allie Reynolds in the first game of the Series, and he responded with a 4-2 victory over New York. Second baseman Jackie Robinson, center fielder Duke Snider and shortstop Pee Wee Reese all hit Brooklyn homers in that contest, and third baseman Gil McDougald hit one for the Yankees. In the second game, Vic Raschi beat Carl Erskine, 7-1, pitching a three-hitter, and the Yankees had tied the Series.

Preacher Rowe was the Brooklyn pitcher in the third game, facing Eddie Lopat. Despite Yankee home runs by catcher Yogi Berra and pinch-hitter Johnny Mize, Brooklyn came away with a 5-3 win, after Berra allowed two runs on a passed ball in the ninth. It was Reynolds and Black again in the fourth game, and this time Reynolds was a 2-0 winner, although both men pitched stylish four-hitters. First baseman Mize hit a home run to produce the Yankees' first score.

Erskin was back to start the fifth game, this time against Ewell Blackwell. He had a shaky outing for a while, giving up five runs in the fifth inning, including Mize's third homer of the Series. But he settled down and retired the last 19 men who faced him. The Dodgers scored three runs in the fifth, two of them from a home run by Snider, then tied the game in the seventh on a single by Snider. Snider nailed down the game in the ninth with a run-producing double off reliever Johnny Sain, who was the loser of the game, 6-5.

Snider continued tearing up opposing pitchers in the sixth game when he hit two more home runs. But

OPPOSITE: Yankee catcher Yogi Berra and umpire Art Passarella look on as Dodger Duke Snider belts his fourth homer for the Series and his second of the game in the eighth inning of the sixth contest. Despite his efforts, the Yankees took the game, 3-2.

ABOVE: Rookie Joe Black, shown here pitching in the ninth inning, hurled the Dodgers to a 4-2 win in the 1952 Series opener.

ABOVE RIGHT: Yankee southpaw Ed Lopat delivering a pitch during game three. Two Dodger runs scored in the ninth on a passed ball, and the Yankees lost, 5-3.

these were matched by homers from Berra and center fielder Mickey Mantle. The Yankees won the game, 3-2; Raschi was the winner and Billy Loes was the loser.

Lopat started against Black in the final game. Both clubs scored one run in the fourth, and then both tallied another in the fifth. The Yankees went ahead on Mantle's homer in the sixth, and went on to win the game, 4-2, and yet another Series, four games to three.

1953

New York Yankees 4, Brooklyn Dodgers 2

The Yankees rolled over the rest of the American League in 1953 to take an unprecedented fifth straight championship under Casey Stengel. It was the easiest pennant of all five, since the Bombers had one 18-game winning streak that all but ended the race. The Dodgers also had an easy road to the National League flag, taking the pennant by a whopping 13 games.

Allie Reynolds started the first game of the World Series for the Yankees, facing Carl Erskine, and the Yankees scored four runs in the first inning. In the fifth, second baseman Junior Gilliam homered for the Dodgers, but catcher Yogi Berra matched that with a home run of his own in the bottom of the inning. Brooklyn came back in the sixth, scoring three runs on a homer by first baseman Gil Hodges, a single by third baseman Billy Cox and a pinch-hit homer by George Shuba. The Dodgers tied the game in the seventh, but the Yankees came back with a run in their half of the inning and three more in the eighth to win, 9-5. The winner was Johnny Sain and the loser Clem Labine, both in relief.

Two southpaws, Preacher Rowe for the Dodgers and Eddie Lopat for the Yankees, faced each other in the second game. Even though Rowe gave up but five hits, he was beaten, 4-2. Manager Chuck Dressen of Brooklyn, two games down, had no choice but to start Erskine once more in the third game, and what a choice this turned out to be. Erskine battled Vic Raschi all the way, but he distinguished himself by striking out 14 Yankees, setting a new World Series record and helping his team achieve a 3-2 victory.

In the fourth game, the Dodgers tied up the Series with a 7-3 win after scoring three runs in the first inning off Whitey Ford. Dodger pitcher Billy Loes pretty much held the Yankees in check until the ninth inning, when the Bombers started a rally. But Clem Labine came in to stifle it after one run had scored. The fifth game was a slugfest, with Mantle hitting a grand slam homer, and second baseman Billy Martin, left

OPPOSITE: Yankees Joe Collins (15), Hank Bauer (9) and Yogi Berra (8) greet Mickey Mantle at home plate after scoring on his grand slam homer in the third inning of game five. The Yanks took the game, 11-7, as a Series record was set when both teams combined for 47 total bases.

ABOVE LEFT AND RIGHT: Sequence shots depict the victory scene in the bottom of the ninth in the '53 Series' sixth and final game. With the score tied at 3-3, Yankee Billy Martin's hit brings home Hank Bauer from third with the winning run. Both Bauer and Martin are surrounded by jubilant teammates celebrating their World Series victory over Brooklyn.

fielder Gene Woodling and third baseman Gil McDougald all hitting home runs. The Yankees went on to win, 11-7. Jim McDonald was the winner and Johnny Podres was the loser.

The sixth game pitted Erskine against Ford. And it was a close contest. New York scored two in the first inning and one in the second. In the sixth, the Dodgers scored one run and two more in the top of the ninth to tie the score. But in the bottom of the ninth, right fielder Hank Bauer walked, Berra lined out, Mantle beat out an infield hit and Martin singled in Bauer for the winning run. The Yankees won, 4-3, and took a record-breaking fifth straight World Series, four games to two.

1954

New York Giants 4, Cleveland Indians 0

Ironically, the New York Yankees won more games in 1954 than in any other single year in Casey Stengel's tenure as manager, with a record of 103-51, but it was not good enough. An inspired Cleveland Indian team under manager Al Lopez broke the American League record by winning 111 games and losing only 43. The superb Indian pitching staff included two 23-game winners, Bob Lemon and Early Wynn. Mike Garcia (19-8) and 35-year-old Bob Feller (13-3) rounded out the intimidating pitching staff.

In the National League it was the New York Giants who came out on top, managed by Leo Durocher. Center fielder Willie Mays had come out of the Army stronger than when he went in. Sparking the club, he hit .345, hit 41 home runs and batted in 110 runs, winning the Most Valuable Player Award in the league. The Giants finished five games ahead of the Dodgers.

In the first game, Sal Maglie of the Giants was pitted against Lemon, and fell behind, 2-0, in the first inning when left fielder Al Smith was hit by a pitch, second baseman Bobby Avila singled and first baseman Vic Wertz tripled. In the third, the Giants tied up the contest on singles by first baseman Whitey Lockman and shortstop Alvin Dark, followed by right fielder Don Mueller's force-out, a walk to Mays and a single by third baseman Hank Thompson. In the eighth inning, Mays made a spectacular catch that many regard as the greatest in Series history. With the score tied 2-2, two Indians on and nobody out, Mays caught Wertz's 460-foot drive over his shoulder and returned it to the infield so fast that neither base runner could advance, turning a seemingly certain triple into a long, noisy out. With one out in the tenth, Mays walked and immediately stole second. Thompson was walked intentionally and Dusty Rhodes was sent in as a pinch-hitter for Monte Irvin. He sent a 260-foot homer into the stands to win the game for the Giants, 5-2.

RIGHT: The Giants' Davey Williams is safe at first as teammate Dusty Rhodes takes out Indian Bobby Avila to break up a double play in game three. Rhodes' pinch-hit single drove in two runs in the third inning and the Giants went on to win, 6-2.

OPPOSITE: Cleveland's lead-off batter Al Smith hits a home run on the first pitch of the Series' second game, at the Polo Grounds.

Johnny Antonelli faced Wynn in the second game. His first pitch was a home run ball to left fielder Al Smith, but that was it for the Indians. Antonelli settled down and in the fifth inning Mays walked, Thompson singled and Rhodes once again batted for Irvin. He hit a bloop single that scored Mays to tie the game. Following this, second baseman Davey Williams struck out, catcher Wes Westrum walked, Antonelli grounded to second – forcing Westrum – but Thompson scored on the play. That was all the Giants needed, but Rhodes put icing on the 3-1 win with a homer in the seventh inning.

Ruben Gómez started the third game for the Giants, and he and reliever Hoyt Wilhelm combined in a four-hitter against Garcia. The game ended 6-2 Giants, and Rhodes was a hero again with a two-run pinch single in the third inning.

It was Don Liddle for the Giants against Lemon in the fourth game. Lemon was knocked out in the fifth inning and Hal Newhouser failed in relief as the Giants took a 7-0 lead. That was the ball game, although Cleveland managed to score three runs in the fifth inning and one in the seventh. The Giants had swept the Series, four games to none, with this 7-4 win.

1955

Brooklyn Dodgers 4, New York Yankees 3

The Dodgers won 22 of their first 24 games in 1955, opening up a nine-and-a-half game lead by the end of the season's first month. They never dropped out of first place, and finished 13 and a half games in front of the Milwaukee Braves, clinching the flag on 8 September, the earliest date in National League history. American League fans enjoyed an exciting four-way contest among the Yankees, White Sox, Indians and Red Sox. The Yankees put on a remarkable finishing run, winning 15 consecutive games, ending the season three games in front of the Indians.

Don Newcombe was selected by Brooklyn manager Walter Alston to start the Series, and Casey Stengel chose Whitey Ford. Newk was knocked out in the sixth inning with the Yankees ahead, 6-3. The game ended 6-5, and the hero was first baseman Joe Collins, a .234 hitter during the season, who hit two home runs in the contest. Tommy Byrne was the winning pitcher for the Yankees in the second game, beating Billy Loes, 4-2, on a five-hitter.

The Dodgers snapped back in the third game, winning it 8-3 behind Johnny Podres. Podres had a puny 9-10 season record, but in this game he scattered seven hits to beat Bob Turley. The Brooklynites won the fourth game to tie the Series. Clem Labine was the winner over Don Larsen in the 8-5 affair.

Dodger center fielder Duke Snider hit two homers in the fifth game to lead his teammates to a 5-3 victory over the Yankees. Roger Craig was the winner over Bob Grim. In the sixth game, the Yankees once again scored all their runs in one inning – five of them in the first – with Ford beating Karl Spooner in this 5-1 complete game victory.

So the Series went down to a seventh, deciding game. It was Podres all the way, scattering eight hits in a 2-0 shutout, and beating Grim. Oddly enough, Byrne, Grim and Bob Turley limited the Dodgers to five hits, but that was enough, as Dodger left fielder Sandy Amoros saved the game in the sixth with a spectacular catch of a Berra fly ball. The Yankees had finally been dethroned, losing the Series four games to three, and Brooklyn had won its first Series. Also for the first time, a World Series Most Valuable Player was selected, and Podres won it hands down.

OPPOSITE TOP: Dodger southpaw Johnny Podres winds up to pitch in the seventh game. Podres shut out the Yanks.

BELOW: Dodger speedster Jackie Robinson slides safely under Yankee Yogi Berra's tag on a steal home in the eighth inning of the Series opener, at Yankee Stadium.

OPPOSITE BOTTOM: Dodger left fielder Sandy Amoros makes a spectacular catch of a Berra fly in game seven.

1956

New York Yankees 4, Brooklyn Dodgers 3

The Brooklyn Dodgers won the pennant again in 1956, but only after taking the race down to the last day of the season. On that day, Don Newcombe won his twenty-seventh game against the Pittsburgh Pirates, permitting the Dodgers to nose out the Milwaukee Braves. On the other hand, the New York Yankees breezed to the American League championship. They moved into first place on 16 May and were never headed. The season ended with the Bronx Bombers nine games ahead of the Cleveland Indians.

Yankee manager Casey Stengel started Whitey Ford in the first game of the Series, and Walter Alston chose Sal 'The Barber' Maglie. Maglie got off to a bad start by giving up two runs in the first inning, but then he settled down, giving up only seven more hits and striking out 10. In the second inning, the Dodgers struck back with a homer by third baseman Jackie Robinson, a single by first baseman Gil Hodges and a double by right fielder Carl Furillo, which tied the score. And in the third, singles by shortstop Pee Wee Reese and center fielder Duke Snider, plus a homer by Hodges, gave the Dodgers the win, 6-3.

Don Larsen of the Yankees started against Newcombe in the second game. By the time the game was over, the Dodgers had used three pitchers and the Yankees seven (a Series record). Brooklyn was behind, 6-0, going into the bottom half of the second inning, but slashed back with six runs of their own in that inning. The Dodgers then went on to score seven more runs to the Yankees' two tallies to win, 13-8, in this three-hour-and-26-minute game – the longest in Series history. Don Bessent was the winner and the loser was Tom Morgan.

Moving to Yankee Stadium, the Bombers proceeded to dominate. Ford returned to the mound and defeated Roger Craig, 5-3, in the third game. In the fourth game, Yankee pitcher Tom Sturdivant scattered

New York Yankees 4, Brooklyn Dodgers 3

116

six hits to beat Carl Erskine, 6-2. Then came the history-making fifth game.

Don Larsen was the starter for the Yankees, and Maglie was the Dodger pitcher. It was a pitchers' duel, with Maglie allowing only five hits and giving up but two runs. Larsen, however, was perfect that day. Going into the ninth inning, not a single Dodger had made it to first base. Furillo opened the last inning by flying out. Then catcher Roy Campanella grounded to second baseman Billy Martin, who threw Campy out at first. Dale Mitchell came to the plate to pinch-hit for Maglie. The count went from 1-0 to 1-1 to 1-2. Mitchell fouled off the next pitch. Larsen reared back and delivered a called third strike to register the only perfect game ever thrown in a World Series.

The Dodgers came back in the sixth game to win in 10 innings, 1-0, as Clem Labine beat Bob Turley. But the Yankees killed the Dodgers in the final game, 9-0, with Johnny Kucks defeating Newcombe. The Series was over with the Bombers winning four games to three. Larsen, of course, was the Series MVP.

OPPOSITE AND LEFT: The Yankees' Don Larsen embraces catcher Yogi Berra after hurling the first Series no-hitter and a perfect game in the fifth contest against the Dodgers, on 8 October 1956.

TOP: Don Larsen, making World Series history as he pitches in game five. Larsen threw 97 pitches as the Yankees beat Brooklyn, 2-0.

1957

Milwaukee Braves 4, New York Yankees 3

The first half of the 1957 season had found the New York Yankees in third place, playing without verve. Then they came to life, won 10 straight games, and moved into first place on 30 June. They finished the season eight games ahead of the Chicago White Sox. In the National League, manager Fred Haney's Milwaukee Braves, who had lost the pennant by a single game the year before, bounced back and finished the season eight games ahead of the second-place St Louis Cardinals, mostly on slick pitching and the hitting of the young center fielder, Henry Aaron, who had just been named Most Valuable Player in the National League.

Whitey Ford of the Yankees was sent in by manager Casey Stengel to open the Series against Warren Spahn, and he did handsomely. He scattered five hits and it wasn't until the seventh inning that the Braves were able to score a run when left fielder Wes Covington doubled and second baseman Red Schoendienst singled. The Yankees won, 3-1.

Lew Burdette was the starter for the Braves in the second game, and was masterful against the Yankees' Bobby Shantz. In this 4-2 Milwaukee win, the Braves scored their winning runs in the fourth. With the score tied, 2-2, first baseman Joe Adcock and right fielder Andy Pafko singled. Covington singled to left center. Adcock scored and Yankee third baseman Tony Kubek, a rookie, missed the relay, letting Pafko score.

The third contest was the opener in Milwaukee, and Milwaukean Kubek had a field day in front of the people in his hometown. He homered in the first inning and the seventh, and was instrumental in the Yankees' 12-3 victory. Brave starter Bob Buhl was knocked out in the Yankees' three-run first inning. The winner was Don Larsen, who relieved Bob Turley in the second inning.

It was Spahn against Tom Sturdivant in the fourth game. The Yankees went ahead, 1-0, in the first inning, but the Braves came back in the fourth with four runs on homers by Aaron and first baseman Frank Torre. After the Yanks scored three runs in the ninth to tie the score, the game went into extra innings. In the tenth the Bombers scored a run, but the seemingly unphased Braves came back with three in the bottom of the tenth on third baseman Eddie Mathews' home run. The game ended 7-5 – the winner was Spahn and the loser was Bob Grim in relief.

In the fifth game it was Burdette against Ford in a real pitchers' duel. With two outs in the Braves' half of the sixth inning, Eddie Mathews beat out a ground ball, Aaron singled and Adcock singled – and that was the only run in the ball game, with the Braves winning, 1-0.

Turley faced Ernie Johnson in the sixth game, which the Yankees won to tie up the Series by a score of 3-2. All the runs in the contest were scored on homers. Catcher Yogi Berra had a two-run clout in the third inning, Torre hit one in the fifth and Aaron banged another in the seventh. In the seventh, right fielder Hank Bauer belted the deciding round-tripper.

The final game of the Series was Burdette's when he shut out five Yankee pitchers, 5-0, scattering seven hits along the way. The Braves had won the Series four games to three, and Burdette, with his three wins, was the obvious choice for Most Valuable Player.

ABOVE: Sequence shots depict the Braves' Eddie Mathews hitting the tenth-inning home run that won the 1957 Series' fourth game.

OPPOSITE TOP: Milwaukee's Lew Burdette pitching in the ninth inning of game five, shutting down the Yankees, 1-0.

OPPOSITE BOTTOM: Starting pitchers for the Series opener, Yankee Whitey Ford and Brave Warren Spahn, shake hands.

1958

New York Yankees 4, Milwaukee Braves 3

The 1958 season found the National League without a team in either New York or Brooklyn. The Giants were playing in San Francisco and the Dodgers in Los Angeles. In the league, it was once more the Milwaukee Braves who won the pennant, finishing eight games ahead of the second-place Pittsburgh Pirates. The Yankees gained their fourth straight American League flag – their ninth in 10 years, with Casey Stengel tying Connie Mack's record for managing nine league champions. The Yanks ended up 10 games ahead of the Chicago White Sox.

In the first game of the Series, Warren Spahn of the Braves won a nifty 4-3 extra-inning game, beating Ryne Duren, who was in relief of starter Whitey Ford. Trailing 3-2, the Braves tied the game in the eighth, and went on to win it in the tenth on singles by first baseman Joe Adcock, catcher Del Crandall and center fielder Billy Bruton.

Lew Burdette was the Braves' pitcher in the second game, and he faced Bob Turley. The Yankees did score one run in the first inning, but the game was never in doubt after the Braves blasted back in the bottom of the first with seven runs. The game ended with a score of 13-5. Burdette not only scattered a mere seven hits, but he himself hit a three-run homer in that fateful first inning.

Right fielder Hank Bauer put on a batting show in the third game, driving in all four Yankee runs. Starter Don Larsen and reliever Ryne Duren of the Yanks were also outstanding, giving up but four hits in the game, shutting out Bob Rush, 4-0.

Spahn was back for the Braves in the fourth contest, and he threw a magnificent two-hitter to shut out Ford, 3-0. But that was it for Milwaukee. In the fifth game, Turley beat Burdette, 7-0. Then Duren beat Spahn, 4-3, in 10 hard-fought innings, with Turley coming in to save the game. In the final game Larsen

OPPOSITE TOP: The Braves' southpaw Warren Spahn winds up in game four. Spahn pitched a two-hitter, helping his team down the Yanks, 3-0.

OPPOSITE BOTTOM: Milwaukee's Hank Aaron watches his long fly-out in game five. Aaron batted .333 for the Series.

LEFT: Yankee Bob Turley lets one fly during the Series' fifth game. Allowing only five hits, Turley shut down the Braves, 7-0.

pitched against Burdette until he was replaced by Turley in the second inning. Going into the eighth inning the score was tied, 2-2, but New York erupted for four runs to win, 6-2, making the Yankees the first team since 1925 to win the Series after being down three games to one. Turley, with his two wins and one save, was voted the Most Valuable Player of the Series.

1959

Los Angeles Dodgers 4, Chicago White Sox 2

The 1959 National League pennant race was a three-way fight among the Los Angeles Dodgers, the Milwaukee Braves and the San Francisco Giants, with the Giants leading by two games in the final week. As the Giants slipped, the Braves and Dodgers added steam, ending the season tied and forcing the third pennant playoff in National League history. The Dodgers, in their third playoff appearance, won the first game in Milwaukee and wrapped up the flag in the best two out of three series by winning in Los Angeles, with a heroic three-run rally in the bottom of the ninth, and another in the bottom of the twelfth, for a final score of 6-5.

The fight for top place in the American League centered on the Chicago White Sox and the Cleveland Indians. Chicago manager Al Lopez relied on outstanding pitching, speed and defense to sweep a four-game series at Cleveland beginning on 28 August. That broke the Indians' back, and the Sox ended the season with a five-game lead.

The weak-hitting Sox overwhelmed the Dodgers in the first game of the Series, 11-0, with Early Wynn defeating Roger Craig. In the game, first baseman Ted Kluszewski hit two homers and went three for four. This tied the Sox with the 1934 St Louis Cardinals for the most one-sided shutout in World Series history.

The Dodgers came back to win the second game, 4-3, with Johnny Podres beating Bob Shaw. It was a game of home runs. The Sox had jumped off to a 2-0 lead in the first inning. The first run for the Dodgers came in the fifth, by way of a home run by second baseman Charley Neal. In the seventh, pinch-hitting for Podres, Chuck Essegian hit a homer to tie the score, and after third baseman Jim Gilliam walked, Neal hit his second round-tripper.

Don Drysdale pitched for the Dodgers in the third game, and faced Dick Donovan. The game was a

LEFT: Dodger Gil Hodges blasts the eighth-inning home run in game four that broke the 4-4 tie and put his team on top of the White Sox to stay.

RIGHT: White Sox outfielder Al Smith gets doused when an excited fan knocks a cup of beer off the ledge, adding insult to injury as Dodger Charley Neal's homer sails into the stands in the fifth inning of game two.

nightmare for loser Donovan, who finished the sixth inning having given up only one hit and issuing no walks. The Dodgers won, 3-1, after the Sox had wasted 12 hits to score a single tally.

The fourth game was close, with the Dodgers winning, 4-3, on a homer by first baseman Gil Hodges in the eighth inning. The winning pitcher was Larry Sherry, in relief of Craig, and the loser was Gerry Staley, the fourth Chicago pitcher. Chicago came back in the fifth game, scoring one run in the fourth inning and hanging on for a 1-0 win. Although outhit 9-5, the Sox won on a combination of three pitchers – Shaw, Billy Pierce and Donovan – the first such win in World Series history. The loser was Sandy Koufax.

The sixth game was no contest, as the Sox scored their first three runs in the fourth inning, when the Dodgers already had scored eight times. The game ended at 9-3, with the winner Sherry and the loser Wynn. Los Angeles had won the Series four games to two, and the Most Valuable Player was Sherry, with his two victories and two saves.

BELOW: Ace Dodger reliever Larry Sherry in action in the Series finale. Sherry relieved Johnny Podres in the fourth inning and shut down the White Sox for a 9-3 win, gleaning two wins and two saves in the Series.

1960

Pittsburgh Pirates 4, New York Yankees 3

The 1960 season found the New York Yankees pulling themselves together after the previous season's slump. They battled the Baltimore Orioles for quite a while during the season, but won 15 straight games toward the end of the season to finish eight games ahead in first place, giving Casey Stengel his tenth win in 12 seasons. When the season began, no one would have picked the Pittsburgh Pirates to win the National League flag. On paper, both the Milwaukee Braves and the Los Angeles Dodgers had better teams. But the Pirates did have right fielder Roberto Clemente, who hit .314; shortstop Dick Groat, who hit .325; and a great pitching staff. Under manager Danny Murtaugh they ended the season seven games ahead of the Braves.

In the first game of the Series, it was Vern Law pitching for the Pirates against Art Ditmar. Yankee right fielder Roger Maris hit a home run in the first inning, but the Pirates scored three in the bottom of the first. The Bucs were never headed and won the game, 6-4. The second game was hardly a contest of finesse, when the Bronx Bombers came back with a 19-hit attack that included two home runs by center fielder Mickey Mantle. The Pirates also had a field day at the plate, getting 13 hits, but they were unable to capitalize on them. After the carnage was over, the Yanks had posted a 16-3 victory, with Bob Turley the winner and Bob Friend the loser.

New York continued beating up on Pittsburgh in the third game, winning it 10-0 behind Whitey Ford, with Wilmer 'Vinegar Bend' Mizell the loser. Second baseman Bobby Richardson led the attack, driving in a record-breaking six runs on a grand slam homer and a two-run single. Pittsburgh was down but not out. In the fourth game they dragged themselves up from the floor and beat New York, 3-2. Vern Law, a 20-game winner during the season, triumphed over Ralph Terry.

LEFT: New York Yankee manager Casey Stengel watches the Pittsburgh Pirates take an early lead in the first inning of the 1960 World Series opener at Forbes Field. The Pirates scored three times that inning, and went on to defeat four Yankee pitchers, 6-4.

OPPOSITE: In the seventh inning of the Series' second game, Yankee slugger Mickey Mantle connects with a low, outside fast ball from Pirate pitcher Joe Gibbon for a three-run homer. Together with his fifth-inning homer, Mantle had five RBI's to lead the Yanks to a 16-3 victory.

BELOW: Pirate Bill Mazeroski is met by third base coach Frank Oceak and excited fans as he rounds the bases after belting the Series-winning home run in the bottom of the ninth inning of game seven. Pittsburgh's 10-9 win over the Yankees clinched their first world championship in 35 years.

The Pirates called in Harvey Haddix to pitch the fifth game, while the Yankees countered with Ditmar. Pittsburgh out-hit the Yanks 10-5, beating them, 5-2. The Yankees came back in the sixth game to overwhelm the Pirates once again, 12-0, exploding for 17 hits. Ford was the winner, and Friend the loser.

The final game was a donnybrook. Turley started for the Yanks and Law for the Bucs. Pittsburgh scored two runs in the first inning and two in the second. The Yankees scored one run in the fifth and four in the sixth. In the eighth, New York added two more and Pittsburgh added five. Behind 9-7, the Yankees tied the ball game in the ninth with two more runs. But then came the bottom of the inning. Second baseman Bill Mazeroski stepped up to the plate, took one pitch for a ball and then hit the homer that made the Pirates champions of the world by a score of 10-9. The winner was Haddix and the loser was Terry. The Most Valuable Player in the Series was Yankee second baseman Bobby Richardson. The Yanks had scored 55 runs to the Pirates' 27, but lost four games to three.

1961

New York Yankees 4, Cincinnati Reds 1

The 1961 season was a race between the Los Angeles Dodgers and the Cincinnati Reds in the National League. But manager Fred Hutchinson of the Reds had both pitching – Joey Jay with 21 wins and Jim O'Toole with 19 – and hitting – center fielder Vada Pinson (.343) and left fielder Frank Robinson (.323). In the American League, on the other hand, the New York Yankees under freshman manager Ralph Houk were considered to be the strongest Yank team since the awesome 1927 crew. Center fielder Mickey Mantle had finished the season with 54 home runs, and right fielder Roger Maris had broken Babe Ruth's season homer mark with 61. And there was always Whitey Ford, who had a 25-4 season on the mound.

It was Ford against O'Toole in the first game of the Series. Ford pitched a two-hit shutout as catcher Elston Howard hit a homer in the fourth inning and first baseman Bill Skowron did the same in the sixth. That was it for the scoring, the Yankees winning, 2-0. The Reds came back in the second game, winning 6-2, with Jay defeating Ralph Terry. In the fourth inning first baseman Gordon Coleman of the Reds smashed a two-run homer, and the feat was duplicated by catcher Yogi Berra of the Yankees in that same inning. But in the fifth inning, Cincinnati went ahead to stay with a run, followed by another in the sixth and two more in the eighth.

That was to be the Reds' only win in the Series. In the third game, Reds' pitcher Bob Purkey suffered a heart-breaking loss in his six-hitter. Cincinnati had taken a 2-1 lead against starter Bill Stafford in the bottom of the seventh inning, but in the eighth, Yankee pinch-hitter Johnny Blanchard tied the game with a home run. Then in the ninth, Maris hit a home run to give the Yankees a 3-2 win.

ABOVE: Red catcher John Edwards slides into the Red dugout at Crosley Field in the seventh inning of game three as he attempts to catch a Mickey Mantle pop-up.

OPPOSITE: The Reds' Frank Robinson at bat in the fifth and final game. Despite Robinson's three-run homer, the Reds lost the game to the Yankees, 13-5.

RIGHT: Yankee ace Whitey Ford displays the pitching form that gave him a 25-4 record in 1961 as he hurls against Cincinnati in the World Series opener at Yankee Stadium. With Ford's 2-0 shutout of the Reds, he achieved a record eighth World Series victory.

It was Ford's turn again in the fourth game, and he faced O'Toole. Ford and reliever Jim Coates combined to throw a five-hitter and shackle the Reds, 7-0. It was in this game that Ford broke Babe Ruth's record of pitching 29 and two-thirds consecutive scoreless innings. When he won the first game of the Series, he had gone 27 innings without giving up a run. In the fourth game, he went five innings without giving up a run before he injured his ankle.

He thereby set a new World Series record of 32 innings.

The Bombers bombed the Reds in the fifth game, and took the game, 13-5, after scoring five runs in the first inning, with Terry facing Jay. The winner of the debacle was reliever Bud Daly, who came on in the third inning. The Yankees were the Series winners at four games to one, and Ford, of course, was the Most Valuable Player.

1962

New York Yankees 4, San Francisco Giants 3

This was the year of major-league expansion. Taking the field for the first time were the New York Mets and the Houston Colt .45s (renamed the Astros in 1965) in the National League. In the American League, the Washington Senators were permitted to leave town to go to Minnesota and become the Twins, a new franchise was given to Washington, and the Los Angeles Angels were added to the league.

Once again the Yankees rose to the top in the American League, but it took until the final two weeks of the season. The big surprise in the league was the tenacity of the two expansion clubs, both of whom gave New York a run for its money. Once again there was a playoff for the National League pennant – for the fourth time in history. And once again, as with the other three, the Los Angeles Dodgers were involved. This time they lost to the San Francisco Giants, two games to one.

In the first game of the World Series, it was Whitey Ford of the Yankees against Billy O'Dell. The Yanks scored two runs in the first inning, but the Giants tied it up with a run in the second and another in the third. From then on it was all Yankees, and they took the game, 6-2. The game, however, did end Ford's consecutive scoreless inning streak at 33 and two-thirds. The Giants came back to win the second game, 2-0, and both starting pitchers were magnificent – winner Jack Sanford and loser Ralph Terry. Sanford held the Yankees to three hits, and Terry allowed only five before he was relieved in the eighth inning.

Bill Stafford of New York faced Billy Pierce in the third game. The final score was 3-2 Yankees, with the Bronx Bombers scoring all their runs in the seventh inning. It was a pitchers' duel, with the Yankees getting but five hits and the Giants four. A seventh-inning grand slam home run by second baseman Charlie Hiller was the big blow in the fourth game, which the Giants won, 7-3. The Series continued to seesaw as the

OPPOSITE TOP: Teammates congratulate San Francisco's Chuck Hiller as he returns to the dugout after hitting a grand slam home run in the seventh inning of the Series' fourth game. With this first-ever National League Series grand slam, Hiller broke the 2-2 tie and propelled his team to a 7-3 win.

OPPOSITE BOTTOM: Giant pitcher Jack Sanford throws the first pitch of game two to Yankee leadoff batter Tony Kubek. Sanford shut the Yanks down, 2-0, allowing only three hits.

LEFT: New York's Ralph Terry shows his stuff as he pitches the Yankees to their twentieth World Series championship with a four-hit, 1-0 shutout over the Giants in the seventh game.

Yankees took the fifth game, 5-3, with Sanford facing Terry again. The game was in doubt until the eighth inning, when the Yankees scored three runs. The Giants gave it a go in the ninth, scoring a run, but it was too little and too late.

Once again the tables were turned, as the Giants won another squeaker in the sixth game, 5-2, with Pierce beating Ford by pitching a three-hitter. The

final game was a white-knuckle affair, starring Sanford and Terry again. In the fifth inning Yankee first baseman Bill Skowron singled, followed by a single by third baseman Clete Boyer. Skowron scored on a double play, and that was the end of the scoring, with the Yankees winning, 1-0, and taking the Series four games to three. Ralph Terry was the Most Valuable Player.

1963

Los Angeles Dodgers 4, New York Yankees 0

The Los Angeles Dodgers came back from their humiliating defeat in 1962 to take the National League pennant in 1963. But manager Walter Alston's men had to battle down to the wire. At the end, they went into St Louis to face the red-hot Cardinals, and beat the Cards three straight games to win the flag. In the American League, the New York Yankees had little problem, finishing 10 and a half games in front – their largest margin since 1947.

Yankee manager Ralph Houk chose Whitey Ford to face Sandy Koufax in the first game of the Series, but it was all Koufax that day, as he set a new World Series record by striking out 15 Yanks, among them the first five men he faced. The Dodgers climbed all over Ford in the second inning to score four runs – and that was all they needed as the game ended 5-2.

In the second game it was Johnny Podres for Los Angeles against Al Downing. Once again the Dodgers scored all the runs they needed in one inning – the first. Shortstop Maury Wills singled to open the inning and promptly stole second. Jim Gilliam, the third baseman, singled, then took second on the throw from outfield to third base. Center fielder Willie Davis then doubled to score both Wills and Gilliam. From then on it was all downhill for the Yankees as the Dodgers beat them, 4-1.

Big Don Drysdale started the third game for the Dodgers, and he faced Jim Bouton. The game was a cliffhanger, with both pitchers at the top of their form. Drysdale gave up but three hits and Bouton yielded only four before he was taken out for a pinch-hitter in the eighth. In the first inning, Gilliam walked, took second on a wild pitch, and scored when left fielder Tommy Davis singled. The Dodgers held on the rest of the way for a 1-0 victory.

Koufax started the fourth game and the Yankees countered with Ford. When the game was over, Ford

OPPOSITE: Dodger ace Sandy Koufax strikes out a Series-record 15 batters for a 5-2 win in the 1962 Series opener at Yankee Stadium.

ABOVE: Los Angeles' right fielder Frank Howard belts a home run in the Series' fourth and final game in support of Sandy Koufax's pitching as the Dodgers won, 2-1, to blank the Yankees, four games to none.

had pitched a two-hitter and Koufax had scattered six hits. The game was scoreless until the fifth inning, when Dodger right fielder Frank Howard belted a tremendous 42-foot home run. In the seventh Yankee center fielder Mickey Mantle countered with a homer of his own to tie the score. But the Dodgers came back in the bottom of the seventh to score once more, and went on to win the game, 2-1, and sweep the Series. For his two wins, Koufax was named the Most Valuable Player of the Series.

1964

St Louis Cardinals 4, New York Yankees 3

The Yankees, under rookie manager Yogi Berra, came back to win the American League pennant yet another time in 1964. But it had been a close race, and the Yanks finished only one game ahead of the Chicago White Sox and two ahead of the Baltimore Orioles. In the National League, the Philadelphia Phillies breezed into the last two weeks of the season with a six-and-a-half game lead. Then, beginning on 20 September, they lost 10 straight games while Johnny Keane's St Louis Cardinals won eight in a row to beat out the Phillies for the flag by one game.

Whitey Ford opened the Series for the Yankees, facing Ray Sadecki. Ford held on to a 4-2 lead until the Cardinals exploded in the sixth inning with four runs. The game ended with the Cards on top, 9-5. Mel Stottlemyre pitched for the Yankees in the second game against Bob Gibson. Stottlemyre scattered seven hits in fashioning his 8-3 victory. Gibson was great in the beginning, striking out six in the first three innings, but began to waver and had to be taken out late in the game.

The third game was close all the way. Cardinal starter Curt Simmons gave up one run in the second inning, but got a single off Yankee pitcher Bouton to drive in the tying run in the fifth. In the ninth, Simmons was taken out for a pinch-hitter, and Barney Schultz was brought in from the bullpen to pitch for the Cardinals. His first pitch was a knuckle ball to right fielder Mickey Mantle, who promptly hit a home run to win the game, 2-1. The Yankees got to Sadecki for three runs in the first inning of the fourth game. Al Downing held the Cards in check until the sixth, when third baseman Ken Boyer hit a grand slam home run to win the game, 4-3. The winning pitcher was Roger Craig in relief. The hard-fought fifth game went to the Cardinals, 5-2, on a three-run homer by catcher Tim McCarver in the tenth inning. The winner was Gibson, who struck out 13 batters, and the loser was Pete Mikkelson in relief. Stottlemyre had been the starter.

OPPOSITE: In the second inning of the 1964 Series opener, Cardinal Mike Shannon scores on Ray Sadecki's single to right. The Cards went on to win, 9-5.

ABOVE: Yankee Joe Pepitone drives the ball onto the roof at Busch Stadium for a grand slam in game six.

RIGHT: Cardinal Bob Gibson pitching in game five. Gibson struck out 13 batters for a 5-2 victory, then went on to strike out nine in game seven.

The Yankees came back with a vengeance in the sixth game, rocking Cardinal starter Simmons for home runs by Roger Maris and Mickey Mantle on two consecutive pitches. First baseman Joe Pepitone iced the game for the Yanks with a grand slam homer in the eighth. The final score was 8-3, and Bouton was the winning pitcher.

It was Gibson and Stottlemyre in the final game. Although he gave up three home runs in the game, Gibson struck out nine and hung on grimly for a 7-5 win. The Cardinals had won the Series four games to three, and Gibson was named the Most Valuable Player in the Series. Probably the strangest thing coming out of that year's World Series happened to the managers. The day after the Series ended, Keane resigned as Cardinal manager and Berra was fired as Yankee manager, although he had won a pennant in his first year of managing. Four days later, Keane was named Yankee manager and in November Berra went to the Mets as a coach.

1965

Los Angeles Dodgers 4, Minnesota Twins 3

Both the San Francisco Giants and the Los Angeles Dodgers got hot in September – the Dodgers winning 13 in a row and the Giants winning 14 in a row. But the Dodgers hung on and won the pennant by two games. With the Yankees having a less-than-excellent year, the American League flag went to the Minnesota Twins.

The first game of the Series fell on Yom Kippur, a Jewish High Holy Day, and this prevented Dodger ace Sandy Koufax from pitching. So manager Walter Alston selected Don Drysdale to start. Twins' manager Sam Mele countered with Jim Grant. With the score tied 1-1, Minnesota exploded for six runs in the third, which included a three-run homer by shortstop Zoilo Versalles. The game ended with an 8-2 Twin victory. As if it weren't enough to beat Drysdale, the Twins went on to beat Koufax the next day. Jim Kaat was the victor in this 5-1 contest.

Los Angeles got back on track in the third game. Claude Osteen threw a 4-0 shutout, giving up only five hits. The loser was Camilo Pasqual. Then Drysdale and Koufax proved that, although a team might beat both of them once, it was almost impossible for a team to beat them twice. In the fourth contest, Drysdale beat Grant, 7-2, and in game five Koufax pitched a 7-0 shutout over Kaat.

Minnesota tied up the Series three games to three in the sixth game. Grant beat Osteen, 5-1, and after Twin left fielder Bob Allison hit a two-run homer in the fourth inning, Grant hit a three-run home run in the sixth. It was Koufax against Kaat in the final game. In the fourth inning the Dodgers scored two runs on a homer by left fielder Lou Johnson, a double by right fielder Ron Fairly and a single by first baseman Wes Parker. That was all Koufax needed as he held Minnesota to three hits, and the 2-0 triumph won the Series for Los Angeles, four games to three. Koufax nailed down the Most Valuable Player Award for this Series.

LEFT: Twin pitcher Jim Kaat shouts triumphantly after snagging the line drive hit by Dodger Dick Tracewski for the final out of the 1965 Series' game two. Kaat beat the Dodgers, 5-1, at Metropolitan Stadium while setting a record for most putouts by a pitcher in Series play.

OPPOSITE: Dodger ace Sandy Koufax hurls a four-hit shutout over the Twins in game five, striking out 10 batters while walking only one batter for a 7-0 win. Koufax was elected to the Hall of Fame in 1971.

1966

Baltimore Orioles 4, Los Angeles Dodgers 0

The 1966 National League race was fairly tight, right up to the end. The Pittsburgh Pirates looked as if they might take it with great hitting and not so great pitching. The Braves had just settled in Atlanta, but despite great hitting, were rather weak. The San Francisco Giants were a real threat. Despite all this, the Los Angeles Dodgers did it again, finishing a mere one and a half games ahead of the pack. In the American League, the pennant belonged to the Baltimore Orioles. By the end of July, they were in first place by 13 games, and were never headed.

It was Dodger star Don Drysdale who was selected by manager Walter Alston to oppose Dave McNally, helmsman Hank Bauer's choice for the first game. Drysdale was out of the game after two innings, with the score 4-1 Baltimore. McNally also had trouble with his control, walking three straight batters in the third to load the bases. In came reliever Moe Drabowsky, who saved the game for the Orioles. In six and two-thirds innings, he struck out 11 Dodgers, including six straight in the fourth and fifth innings. The game ended with a 5-2 Oriole victory, with Drabowsky the winner.

Dodger Sandy Koufax took the mound in the second game and faced Jim Palmer. During the season, Koufax had gone 27-9 and Palmer was a mere 15-10. But Palmer threw a four-hitter for a 6-0 Oriole win, aided by three Dodger errors in the fifth.

The Series was really over, even if the Dodgers didn't know it. In the third game Claude Osteen of Los Angeles tossed a three-hitter, opposing Wally Bunker, who allowed only six. But the telling blow was a home run by Oriole center fielder Paul Blair, and that was the ball game, Baltimore winning 1-0. The final game ended with exactly the same score. It was McNally and Drysdale again, and both of them pitched four-hitters. Again the game was settled by a home run – this time by right fielder Frank Robinson in the fourth

OPPOSITE: The Orioles' relief pitcher Moe Drabowsky, who relieved Dave McNally in the third inning of the '66 Series opener, fanned 11 in the game – including six consecutive – for a Series record by relief pitchers. His one-hit performance insured a 5-2 win for Baltimore.

LEFT: Baltimore's Paul Blair gets a hero's welcome in the dugout after belting a homer in the fifth inning of game three.

ABOVE: A bit of levity in the locker room as Orioles Hank Bauer (left) and Frank Robinson celebrate after the latter's homer clinched the Series victory for Baltimore.

inning. The Orioles had won the Series four games to none, and Robinson was the Most Valuable Player.

It had been a humiliating World Series for the Dodgers. They lost four straight. They managed to score only two runs in four games, going 33 innings without scoring. They committed six errors – all of them in the second game – while the Orioles went errorless.

1967

St Louis Cardinals 4, Boston Red Sox 3

In the American League the Boston Red Sox rebounded from a next-to-last place finish in 1966 to take the pennant on the last day of the season. In the National League, nothing could stop the St Louis Cardinals. By 15 July, they were in first place by four games. Then their star pitcher, Bob Gibson, had his leg broken by a line drive off the bat of Pittsburgh right fielder Roberto Clemente. That might have marked the end of the Cards, but their former relief pitcher, Nelson Briles, took up the slack and the Cardinals took the flag almost two weeks before the season ended, leaving San Francisco 10 and a half games behind at the finish.

By the time that the Series began, Gibson was back in the lineup, and manager Red Schoendienst chose him to oppose Boston manager Dick Williams' selection, Jose Santiago. Santiago pitched effectively and even hit a home run. But that was the only run that Boston could manage, and Gibson was superb. He pitched a six-hitter and struck out 10 batters to post a 2-1 win.

Jim Lonborg of the Sox faced Dick Hughes in the second game. And he was overwhelming, pitching a one-hitter to shut out the Cardinals, 5-0. The only hit was a double by second baseman Julian Javier in the eighth inning. The Cardinals regained the lead in the Series in the third game. Briles went all the way against Gary Bell and three relief pitchers to win, 5-2.

In the fourth game, Gibson was back again, this time to face Santiago once more. The Boston pitcher was knocked out of the game in the very first inning, when St Louis scored four runs. This time Gibson pitched a five-hitter, as the Cardinals went on to win, 6-0. Lonborg came back in the fifth game, pitching a three-hitter to defeat the Cards, 3-1. Steve Carlton was the loser.

The Red Sox had their hitting shoes on in the sixth game, which they won 8-4, with John Wyatt the win-

OPPOSITE TOP: Cardinal pitcher Nelson Briles delivers the first pitch of game three to Boston's lead-off man, Jose Tartabull, who grounds out to second baseman Julian Javier. Briles held the Red Sox to seven hits for a 5-2 win.

OPPOSITE BOTTOM: In the first inning of the Series opener Cardinal leaf-off batter Lou Brock steals second as shortstop Rico Petrocelli waits for the throw. Brock hit four singles and stole two bases to help his Cards take the win.

LEFT: The grim-faced Cardinal manager Red Schoendienst watches from the dugout as St Louis gets bombed by three Red Sox home runs in the fourth inning of game six. Eight pitchers were not able to stop the Boston attack, as they won, 8-4, to even up the Series at three games each.

ner and Jack Lamabe the loser, both in relief. The Sox's explosive 12-hit attack featured two home runs by shortstop Rico Petrocelli, and one each by left fielder Carl Yastrzemski and center fielder Reggie Smith. By the end of the game, St Louis had used eight pitchers.

The showdown game went to St Louis, 7-2, with Gibson beating Lonborg. The Cardinal pitcher went the distance, allowing only three hits and striking out 10, while helping his own cause by hitting a home run. The World Series was over, with the St Louis Cardinals the winners, four games to three. Bob Gibson, of course, was selected Most Valuable Player.

1968

Detroit Tigers 4, St Louis Cardinals 3

The Detroit Tigers under manager Mayo Smith devoured the American League in 1968, finishing 12 games ahead at the end of the season, largely because of the pitching arm of Denny McLain. McLain's 31-6 record made him the first 30-game winner since Dizzy Dean did it for the 1934 St Louis Cardinals. Needless to say, he was voted both the American League's Most Valuable Player and the Cy Young Award. Red Schoendienst's St Louis Cardinals came right back to take the National League flag, nine games ahead of the San Francisco Giants. The Cardinals' star was once again Bob Gibson, the pitcher who won 22 games during the season, 15 in a row, and 13 of them shutouts. Gibson, too, was voted Most Valuable Player in the National League and won the Cy Young Award.

The first game saw Gibson facing McLain. But it turned out to be no contest. Gibson not only shut out the Tigers, 4-0, but also set a World Series record by striking out 17 batters. Nelson Briles started for the Cardinals in the second game, and he faced Mickey Lolich. Lolich surprised everybody by turning in a six-hit performance, and surprised himself by hitting his first home run in his major-league career. The game ended, 8-1.

In the third game, it was the Cards' turn to explode, which they did, getting 13 hits on their way to a 7-3 victory. Ray Washburn was the winner and Earl Wilson was the loser. St Louis got 13 hits the next day as well, beating the Tigers 10-1 in game four. Once again Gibson had no trouble in beating McLain as he set another World Series record by getting his seventh straight complete game victory.

In the fifth game, Lolich faced Briles for the second time. The Cardinals scored three times in the first inning on a double by left fielder Lou Brock, a single by center fielder Curt Flood, and a homer by first baseman Orlando Cepeda. But Lolich withstood the barrage and allowed no more Cardinal runs. Detroit went

on to score two runs in the fourth and three in the seventh to win, 5-3. Joe Hoerner was the loser in relief.

The Cardinals suffered the worst defeat in their history in the sixth game, with McLain beating Washburn, 13-1. In the third, the Tigers tied a World Series record by scoring 10 runs. The final game pitted Gibson against Lolich, and each pitcher threw scoreless ball for the first six innings. But in the seventh inning the Tigers scored three runs after two were out, and went on to win the game, 4-1, and the Series four games to three. For his three victories, Lolich was named the Series' Most Valuable Player.

OPPOSITE: Cardinal pitcher Bob Gibson fans Detroit's Norm Cash in the Series opener for a Series record sixteenth strikeout. Cash struck out at his next at bat as Gibson shut down the Tigers, 4-0.

ABOVE: Detroit's jubilant pitcher Mickey Lolich is carried off the field by catcher Bill Freehan after beating St Louis in the Series' seventh, deciding game, 4-1.

1969

New York Mets 4, Baltimore Orioles 1

Before the 1969 season began, the two leagues had once again added expansion teams, and had broken up into two separate divisions, the Eastern Division and the Western Division. The National League added the San Diego Padres and the Montreal Expos, and the American League accepted the additions of the Kansas City Royals and the Seattle Pilots. The winners of the two divisions in each league would face each other in a best-of-five playoff.

Gil Hodges' New York Mets were the team of destiny in 1969. The Chicago Cubs were leading the Eastern Division of the National League almost all season and by 13 August, the Mets were nine and a half games out of first place. Then the Mets won 38 of their last 49 games, the Cubs collapsed, and New York finished eight games ahead of the pack. In the Western Division, the winners were the Atlanta Braves. The Mets, who had never finished higher than ninth place, astonished everyone by winning the pennant, beating Atlanta in three straight games – 9-1, 11-6 and 7-4.

Earl Weaver's Baltimore Orioles won the Eastern Division of the American League with a solid 109 victories, ending 19 games in front of the field. In the West, the Minnesota Twins won the title after a season-long fight against the Oakland A's. Then Baltimore won three straight in the playoffs, winning 4-3, 1-0 (both in extra innings) and 11-2.

The pitching opponents in the first game of the World Series were the Mets' Tom Seaver (25-7) and the Orioles' Mike Cuellar (23-11). In the bottom of the first inning the leadoff man, left fielder Don Buford, hit a homer on Seaver's second pitch, and the Orioles went on to win the game, 4-1. Jerry Koosman started for the Mets in the second game, and he faced Dave McNally. Koosman threw for six hitless innings and was nursing a 1-0 lead, the result of first baseman Donn Clendenon's fourth-inning homer, going into the seventh.

But then Baltimore tied the score. After two were out in the ninth, three successive singles by the Mets' third baseman Ed Charles, catcher Jerry Grote and second baseman Al Weis resulted in one run. Koosman had tossed a two-hitter for eight and two-thirds innings, and the Mets had won, 2-1.

Gary Gentry of the Mets faced Jim Palmer of the Orioles in the third game, but the contest belonged to New York center fielder Tommy Agee. He blasted a home run in the first inning. In the fourth, with men on first and second, he raced to the 396-foot sign in left center to make a backhanded

OPPOSITE: The Mets' Don Clendenon smashes a two-run home run in the sixth inning of the Series' fifth and final game. The Mets went on to win the game, 5-3, and the Series.

ABOVE: Baltimore's Mike Cueller hurls the first pitch to open the 1969 World Series.

BELOW: Former Met manager Casey Stengel and manager Gil Hodges embrace after the New Yorkers won the Series.

fingertip catch of a ball that looked like a sure triple. In the seventh, with the bases loaded, he made a seemingly-impossible diving catch of a line shot that would have been a double. By himself, Agee made the difference of six runs in the Mets' decisive 5-0 victory.

It was Seaver facing Cuellar in the fourth game. Clendenon hit a home run in the second inning, and the lead stood up until the Orioles tied it in the ninth. The Mets scored in the tenth to win, 2-1, and the losing pitcher was reliever Dick Hall. It was Koosman and McNally in the fifth game. Koosman survived a three-run shelling in the third inning and ended up pitching a five-hitter. The Mets scored twice in the sixth, tied the game at 3-3 in the seventh, and won it, 5-3, on doubles by left fielder Cleon Jones and right fielder Ron Swoboda in the eighth, plus a pair of Oriole errors by first baseman Boog Powell and reliever Eddie Watt (who became the losing pitcher). The Mets were world champions, winning by four games to one. Clendenon was voted the Most Valuable Player of the Series.

1970

Baltimore Orioles 4, Cincinnati Reds 1

In the American League, the 1970 season did not produce many surprises, with the Orioles again winning the Eastern Division and the Twins winning the Western Division. The Orioles did it with essentially the same team as the year before, ending the season 15 games ahead of the second-place Yankees. The Twins finished nine games ahead of the second-place Oakland A's. And once again the Orioles wiped out the Twins in three straight games.

The National League also had a pair of winners who seemed to have little trouble. The Pittsburgh Pirates won the Eastern Division by five games over the Chicago Cubs, and the Cincinnati Reds left the second-place Los Angeles Dodgers 14 and a half games behind. In the playoffs, the Reds defeated the Pirates in three straight, but close, games, 3-0 (in extra innings), 3-1 and 3-2.

In the first game of the Series, manager Sparky Anderson of the Reds chose Gary Nolan as his starter and manager Earl Weaver of the Orioles picked Jim Palmer. The Reds went right to work on Palmer, scoring a run in the first and two more in the third. Then the Orioles got busy, hitting the long ball. In the fourth inning, first baseman Boog Powell hit a two-run homer, and in the fifth, catcher Elrod Hendricks hit one of his own to tie the score. Third baseman Brooks Robinson put the Orioles ahead with another homer in the seventh. The game ended 4-3.

In the second contest, the Reds once again went out on top, scoring three runs in the first inning and one in the third, routing pitcher Mike Cuellar. Then the Orioles knocked out pitcher Jim McGlothlin in the fourth with five runs, after they had scored one in the third. The Reds added another run in the sixth, but went down to defeat, 6-5. The winner was Tom Phoebus and the loser was Milt Wilcox, both in relief. In the third game the opposing pitchers were Dave McNally for Baltimore and Tony Cloninger for Cincinnati.

LEFT: The Orioles' Brooks Robinson connects for a home run in the seventh inning of the 1970 Series opener at Riverfront Stadium, putting Baltimore ahead to stay.

OPPOSITE TOP: Baltimore's Boog Powell is safe at home in the third inning of game three, despite Red catcher Johnny Bench's attempt to block the plate. This was the Orioles' third tally; they went on to reap a 9-3 victory.

OPPOSITE BOTTOM: Cincinnati's Gary Nolan pitching in the World Series. Nolan was 18-7 in the 1970 regular season.

The Orioles scored two runs in the first inning and were never headed, winning the game, 9-3.

It was Palmer versus Nolan in the fourth game. For the first seven innings it looked as if the Orioles were going to sweep the Series. But in the eighth they saw their 5-3 lead disappear as the Reds scored three times to win the game, 6-5. The winning pitcher was Clay Carroll and the loser was Eddie Watt, both in relief.

Cuellar was back in the fifth game to face Jim Merritt. The Reds immediately leaped off to a three-run lead in the first inning, but that was all they were to get. The Orioles came back with two runs each in the first, second and third innings, and coasted to a 9-3 win, taking the world championship four games to one. Slick-fielding Brooks Robinson was named Most Valuable Player.

1971

Pittsburgh Pirates 4, Baltimore Orioles 3

The National League division winners were the San Francisco Giants in the West, finishing two games ahead of the Los Angeles Dodgers, and in the East, the Pittsburgh Pirates, who finished seven games ahead of the St Louis Cardinals. In the playoffs, the Giants beat the Pirates in the first game, 5-4, but led by first baseman Bob Robertson's four home runs, the Pirates swept the next three, 9-4, 2-1 and 9-5.

In the American League, the Baltimore Orioles won the Eastern Division for the third straight year, leaving the Detroit Tigers behind by 12 games. In the Western Division, the Oakland A's broke away from the pack, with the Kansas City Royals 16 games behind in second place. Baltimore won the playoffs in three games.

The Series opened with Dock Ellis pitching for Danny Murtaugh's Pirates, facing Dave McNally of Earl Weaver's Orioles. The Pirates seemed to be in control when they scored three runs in the second inning, but the Orioles started to claw back in the bottom of the second with a homer by outfielder Frank Robinson. Then came three runs in the third, when Baltimore's Merv Rettenmund blasted a three-run homer, giving the Orioles the lead and sending Ellis to the showers. In the fifth, left fielder Don Buford of Baltimore hit another round-tripper to end the scoring, and the Orioles were the winners, 5-3. When Baltimore wiped out the Pirates, 11-3, in the second game, getting 14 hits, it seemed that they were in the driver's seat in the Series. The winning pitcher was Jim Palmer and the loser was Bob Johnson.

But there was still life in the Pirates, and they came back to win the third game, 5-1, as Steve Blass tossed a masterful three-hitter to beat Mike Cueller. Pittsburgh also won the fourth game, tying the Series at two games each as Bruce Kison, in relief, beat Eddie Watt, also in relief, 4-3. The Pirates then took the lead in the

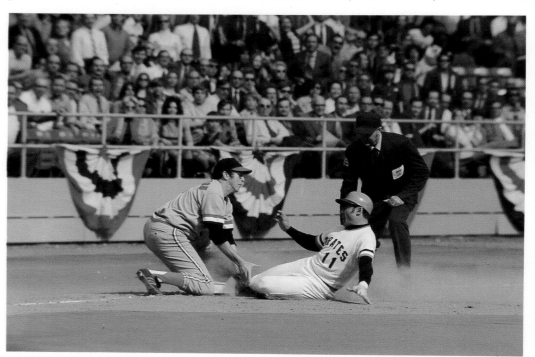

LEFT: The Orioles' stellar third baseman Brooks Robinson applies the tag for a putout in the 1971 Series against the Pittsburgh Pirates. Along with his sparkling performance on the field, Robinson tied a Series record in game two by reaching base in five consecutive at-bats on two walks and three hits.

OPPOSITE: After turning in a 20-win season in 1971, the Orioles' ace Jim Palmer pitched his way to a game two victory in the Series. Palmer pitched nine innings of game six, leaving the game with the score tied; Baltimore won in extra innings.

Series with a 4-0 victory in the fifth game, in which pitcher Nelson Briles was in complete control, pitching a two-hitter to defeat McNally.

Baltimore pulled out a squeaker in the sixth game. After the Pirates had scored one run in the first inning and another in the second, the Orioles started chipping away at the lead, tallying one run in the sixth and one in the seventh, and finally the deciding run in the ninth to win, 3-2. McNally was

the winning pitcher in relief, and starter Bob Miller was the loser.

So it came down to the seventh game, and once again it was Blass against Cuellar. It was a pitchers' duel, with Blass allowing only four hits. It ended with the Pirates winning the game, 2-1, and the Series four games to three. Right fielder Roberto Clemente of the Pirates was named Most Valuable Player.

1972

Oakland Athletics 4, Cincinnati Reds 3

In the 1972 pennant race the Oakland A's repeated in the Western Division of the American League, beating out the Chicago White Sox by five and a half games. The only real contest in either league was in the American League's Eastern Division, where, even as late as Labor Day, four teams – Boston, Baltimore, Detroit and New York – were separated by only half a game. With five games to go in the season, Baltimore was eliminated. With four to go, New York was out, and with three to go, the Red Sox led the Tigers by half a game. Then Detroit faced Boston and took two games out of three, winning the flag. In the playoffs, Oakland won the championship three games to two.

In the National League the Eastern Division champions were the Pittsburgh Pirates, with the Cincinnati Reds winning in the West by 10 and a half games over Houston. The Reds then went on to beat the Pirates in the playoffs, but it took them all five games and a wild pitch by the Pirates' Bob Moose in the bottom of the ninth inning of the final game.

Reds' manager Sparky Anderson opened the Series with pitcher Gary Nolan, who faced manager Dick Williams' choice, Ken Holtzman. Oakland catcher Gene Tenace stunned the baseball world by hitting home runs in his first two times at bat, thus batting in three runs – all the A's needed to win the game, 3-2.

In the second game Jim 'Catfish' Hunter was the starter for the A's and Ross Grimsley went for the Reds. Oakland scored all the runs they needed in the second and third innings to win, 2-1. The Reds came back in the third game when Jack Billingham tossed a three-hitter against John 'Blue Moon' Odom. In the seventh inning a single by Reds' first baseman Tony Perez, third baseman Denis Menke's sacrifice and a single by right fielder Cesar Geronimo gave Cincinnati the win, 1-0.

In the fourth game the Reds were ahead, 2-1, going into the bottom of the ninth inning. But then the A's

hit successive singles by pinch-hitter Gonzalo Marquez, Tenace (who had hit a homer in the fifth), pinch-hitter Don Mincher and pinch-hitter Angel Mangual. The game was over and the A's had won, 3-2. The winning pitcher was Rollie Fingers and the loser was Clay Carroll, both in relief.

The fifth game was a wild affair. The Reds went out in front on a first-pitch-of-the-game homer by Pete Rose, then fell behind in the second, and finally came back to give Grimsley (the fifth of six Reds' pitchers) the 5-4 decision over Fingers (the second of three Oakland pitchers).

The Reds evened the Series in the sixth game, pounding Vida Blue and three other pitchers for 10 hits to win the game, 8-1. Grimsley was the winner in relief. The deciding seventh game was a confrontation between Odom and Billingham. The A's won, 3-2 – their first Series title since 1930. Tenace, who singled and doubled to bat in two runs in the game, was voted the Series' Most Valuable Player.

LEFT: The Athletics' relief pitcher Rollie Fingers pitched in six 1972 Series games, for a win, a loss and two saves.

OPPOSITE TOP LEFT: Oakland's John 'Blue Moon' Odom struck out 11 and allowed just three hits in game three, but the Reds won it, 1-0.

OPPOSITE TOP RIGHT: Oakland's left fielder Joe Rudi makes a spectacular game-saving catch of Denis Menke's drive in the ninth inning of game two.

OPPOSITE BOTTOM: The Reds' Tony Perez connects for a single in the seventh inning of game three, then later scored the winning run.

1973

Oakland Athletics 4, New York Mets 3

The Mets pulled a repeat miracle of the 1969 season in 1973. Under manager Yogi Berra, they were in last place on 30 August. But on the last day of the season, they needed only a split with the Chicago Cubs in a double-header to win the National League Eastern Division. And split they did, taking the flag with a puny .509 won-lost percentage, the lowest of any pennant winner in baseball history. In the West, the Cincinnati Reds made a final charge and took the championship by three and a half games over the Los Angeles Dodgers. The Mets took the pennant in three out of five games from the Reds.

The Oakland A's won the Western Division championship in the American League once again. In the East it was the Baltimore Orioles who ended in first, eight games ahead of the Boston Red Sox. The playoffs also went five games, with the A's emerging triumphant.

Manager Dick Williams selected Ken Holtzman to open the Series for Oakland, and he faced Jon Matlack. In six innings Matlack gave up only three hits, but they all came in the third inning, after two men were out. Then Holtzman doubled, shortstop Bert Campaneris got to first on an error and stole second, and was driven home by left fielder Joe Rudi's single. The other hit was a meaningless single by third baseman Sal Bando. That was all Oakland needed, and they won, 2-1.

In the second game, a record was set when 11 pitchers trudged to the mound. The Mets got 15 hits and made one error; the A's got 13 hits and made five errors. When the dust had cleared, after 12 innings, it was 10-7 for the Mets, with Tug McGraw the winner and Rollie Fingers the loser, both in relief. In game three it was Tom Seaver of the Mets facing Catfish Hunter. New York got off to a two-run lead in the first inning, but that was all that they would score. Oakland scored one run each in the sixth, eighth and eleventh innings

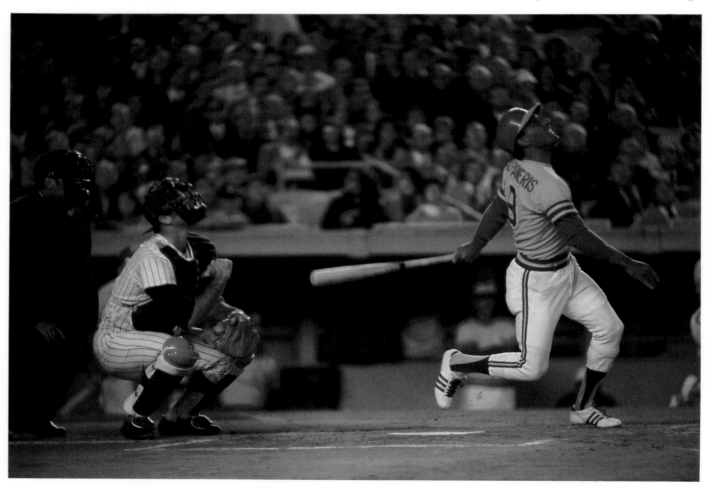

The Athletics' Bert Campaneris hits a sky ball in the '73 Series. Companeris got the decisive hit in the eleventh inning of game three, bringing in the winning run. He had another moment in the sun when he hit a two-run homer in the seventh, deciding game.

RIGHT: The Mets' southpaw Jerry Koosman winds up for a pitch in the '73 Series. In game five Koosman was relieved by Tug McGraw in the seventh inning; between them they allowed but three hits to shut out the A's, 2-0.

BELOW: Oakland's Reggie Jackson at bat in game seven, in which his two-run homer helped the A's secure the championship title. With six RBI's on nine hits, Jackson was voted Series MVP.

for a 3-2 win. The winner was Paul Linblad and the loser was Harry Parker, both in relief.

The Mets' right fielder Rusty Staub had a field day in the fourth game. Staub had four hits, including a home run, plus a walk for a perfect night at the plate, batting in five runs, more than enough for the victory as New York won the game, 6-1. Matlack was the winner and Holtzman the loser. In the fifth game, Jerry Koosman and reliever McGraw threw a three-hitter at the A's, and the Mets won the game, 2-0. The loser was Vida Blue.

It was Seaver against Hunter again in the sixth game. But Oakland outfielder Reggie Jackson got three hits and drove in two runs, which was all the A's needed to win, 3-1. The final game was a disaster for the Mets. Matlack faced Holtzman, but Oakland scored four runs in the third inning and another in the fifth to take the contest, 5-2, winning the championship four games to three. Jackson, who batted in six runs on nine hits, was voted the Most Valuable Player in the Series.

1974

Oakland Athletics 4, Los Angeles Dodgers 1

In the Eastern Division of the National League, the Pittsburgh Pirates managed to squeeze by the St Louis Cardinals by one and a half games. In the Western Division, the Los Angeles Dodgers gained first place in the first week of the season and never looked back, ending up four games ahead of the Cincinnati Reds. In the playoffs, the Dodgers were the winners by three games to one, with Don Sutton pitching brilliantly, winning two of the games while giving up only seven hits.

Alvin Dark was the new manager of the Oakland A's, and they continued their winning ways, beating out the Texas Rangers by five games in the Western Division of the American League. The Baltimore Orioles were also repeaters in the Eastern Division, coming in two games ahead of the New York Yankees. The playoffs went four games, with the A's triumphant, three games to one.

Dodger manager Walter Alston chose Andy Messersmith to face Ken Holtzman in the Series opener. The A's took the lead early when Reggie Jackson homered to lead off the second inning. Holtzman helped his own cause by doubling in the fifth, taking third on a wild pitch, and scoring on shortstop Bert Campaneris' squeeze bunt. (Because of the designated hitter rule, this was Holtzman's first time at bat all year.) The Dodgers scored a run in their half of the fifth. The A's got an insurance run in the eighth, Dodger center fielder Jimmy Wynn hit a home run in the ninth, and the A's had won the game, 3-2. The winner was Rollie Fingers in relief, and the loser was Messersmith.

In game two it was Vida Blue of the A's against the Dodgers' Don Sutton. Going into the top of the ninth inning, the Dodgers had what seemed to be a comfortable 3-0 lead. Then Sutton hit third baseman Sal Bando with a pitch. Jackson doubled and left fielder Joe Rudi singled with two runs scoring. Los Angeles won the squeaker, 3-2. Catfish Hunter of the A's started the third game against Al Downing. The game was

LEFT: The Athletics' Reggie Jackson gets back to first base ahead of Dodger first baseman Steve Garvey's tag on a pick-off attempt during the 1974 World Series.

almost a complete reversal of the previous contest, with the A's going into the eighth inning with a 3-0 lead, whereupon the Dodgers scored once in the eighth and once in the ninth, but came up short to lose, 3-2.

Messersmith and Holtzman once again faced each other in the fourth game. And once again Holtzman helped his own cause – this time with a homer in the third inning. The Dodgers took the lead with two runs in the fourth, but that was all

they would get as Oakland won the game, 5-2. In the fifth game, the A's scored a run in the first and another in the second. Then the Dodgers tied the game in the sixth. In the seventh, Rudi hit the first pitch for a line drive home run, and the A's went on to win the game, 3-2, and the Series four games to one. Blue Moon Odom was the winner and Mike Marshall, in relief, was the loser of the final game. Fingers, with three saves and one win, was voted the Most Valuable Player in the Series.

ABOVE: Oakland's superstar Reggie Jackson takes a mighty cut for a strike during the '74 Series. Jackson's second-inning home run off Andy Messersmith in the Series opener proved to be the difference, as the A's took it, 3-2.

LEFT: A's first baseman Gene Tenace topples over after making a big stretch for the attempted putout as the umpire signals 'safe' in '74 Series play.

153

1975

Cincinnati Reds 4, Boston Red Sox 3

In the American League, it all belonged to Darrell Johnson's Boston Red Sox, who finished four and a half games ahead of the Baltimore Orioles in the Eastern Division. In the West, it was the A's once again, this time by seven games over the Kansas City Royals. But in the pennant playoffs, the A's went down in three straight to the Red Sox.

In the Eastern Division of the National League, the Pittsburgh Pirates took their fifth title in six years, leaving the Philadelphia Phillies six and a half games behind. And in the Western Division, the Cincinnati Reds won 108 games and left the Los Angeles Dodgers 20 games behind in second place. The Reds then rolled over the Pirates in three straight games.

Manager Sparky Anderson of the Reds picked Don Gullett to start the Series against the venerable Luis Tiant. For six innings it was a scoreless game. Then in the seventh, Tiant started a six-run rally with a single, and the Sox triumphed, 6-0. The second game featured Bill Lee of the Sox against Jack Billingham. Boston scored in the first, Cincinnati in the fourth, and Boston made it 2-1 in the sixth. In the ninth, catcher Johnny Bench doubled for the Reds, then after two were out, shortstop Dave Concepción hit a single that scored Bench. Concepción stole second and scored on right fielder Ken Griffey's double. The Reds won the game, 3-2, with Rawley Eastwick the winner and Dick Drago the loser, both in relief.

The Red Sox were down 5-1 at one point in the third game, but tied the score in the top of the ninth. In a disputed call in the bottom of the tenth, the Reds' pinch-hitter Ed Armbrister attempted a sacrifice bunt with Cesar Geronimo on first. Armbrister failed to move away fast enough, and Sox catcher Carlton Fisk bumped into him. Fisk's resultant bad throw allowed Geronimo to get to third and Armbrister took second. Despite a Boston claim of interference, the Red runners stayed put. After an intentional pass to third base-

ABOVE: A controversial play occurred in the tenth inning of game three, when Red Sox catcher Carlton Fisk collided with Cincinnati's Ed Armbrister as he tried to catch the bunt. The baserunner's interference was ruled unintentional, and runners advanced on Fisk's wild throw to second, setting up the Reds' game-winning run.

man Pete Rose and a strikeout by pinch-hitter Merv Rettenmund, second baseman Joe Morgan singled to win the game, 6-5. The winner was Eastwick and the loser was Jim Willoughby, both in relief.

It was Tiant against Fred Norman in the fourth game. Again the aged Cuban was equal to the occasion, winning 5-4. The Reds won the fifth game, 6-2, on two home runs by first baseman Tony Perez and the masterful pitching of Gullett, who had a

RIGHT: In Pete Rose's third Series appearance, in 1975, he led his team in batting average with .370, helping the Reds take the title. Rose batted in two runs and scored three.

LEFT: Red Sox outfielder Fred Lynn trots home after hitting a two-run homer in game six. Carlton Fisk waits to congratulate him; his twelfth-inning blast would later conclude one of baseball's most thrilling World Series games.

two-hitter going into the ninth inning. The loser was Reg Cleveland. Boston tied the Series in the hard-fought sixth game, winning 7-6 in the twelfth inning. The game lasted four hours and one minute, ending at 12:33 AM, with the winner Dick Wise and the loser Pat Darcy, both in relief.

The final game pitted Gullett against Lee, but neither were able to last long. Boston scored three in the third inning, Cincinnati scored two in the sixth

and one in the seventh. In the ninth, Griffey walked, was sacrificed to second, and got to third on an infield out. Rose was walked intentionally. Then Morgan singled Griffey home. The Reds won the game, 4-3, and the Series four games to three – their first world championship in 35 years. In the final game the winner was Clay Carroll and the loser was Jim Burton, both in relief. Pete Rose was voted the Series' Most Valuable Player.

1976

Cincinnati Reds 4, New York Yankees 0

Once again the Cincinnati Reds swept the Western Division of the National League, leaving the Los Angeles Dodgers 10 games behind. In the Eastern Division, the Philadelphia Phillies beat out the Pittsburgh Pirates, but fell to the Reds in the playoffs, three games to none. In the American League, the Western Division was won by the Kansas City Royals, who came out ahead of the Oakland A's by two games. Inspired by manager Billy Martin's aggressive style, the New York Yankees ended up in first place in the East, leading the Baltimore Orioles by 10 and a half games. The league playoffs went the full five games, and the fifth game was won by Yankee first baseman Chris Chambliss with a ninth-inning home run.

Cincinnati manager Sparky Anderson chose Don Gullett to start the first game, and he faced Doyle Alexander. In the bottom of the first inning, Cincinnati's second baseman, Joe Morgan, hit a home run. The Yankees tied the score in the second, and that was it for the Bronx Bombers. The Reds went on to win the game, 5-1.

Fred Norman was on the mound for the Reds in the second game, and he was opposed by Catfish Hunter. The Reds jumped off to a 3-0 lead in the second inning, but the Yankees came back with a run in the fourth and tied the score with two more in the seventh. After two men were out in the ninth, a throwing error by Yankee shortstop Fred Stanley allowed right fielder Ken Griffey to take second. Morgan was intentionally passed so that Hunter could pitch to righthanded-hitting first baseman Tony Perez. But Perez crossed them up by singling in the winning run to defeat the Yanks, 4-3.

Dock Ellis of the Yankees faced Pat Zachry in the third game, but he was knocked out of the box with one out in the fourth inning, having given up four runs. The Reds went on to win, 6-2. The fourth game sealed

LEFT: The Reds' first baseman Tony Perez at bat in the 1976 World Series. Perez' .313 batting performance included the game-winning RBI in game two, when he singled in Ken Griffey.

OPPOSITE TOP: Yankee baserunner Chris Chambliss is out at second as Red second baseman throws to first for the attempted double play, and shortstop Dave Concepcion looks on.

OPPOSITE BOTTOM: New York's Chris Chambliss at bat, with the Reds' Johnny Bench catching. Chambliss, who batted .313 for the Series, tried to start a game four rally with his first-inning RBI, but the Reds put seven runs across for a decisive victory.

the doom of the Yankees. New York opened the scoring in the first inning on a single by catcher Thurman Munson and a double by Chambliss. But the Reds came back with three runs in the fourth on a walk to Morgan (who stole second), a single by left fielder George Foster, and a home run by catcher Johnny Bench, who would hit two home runs that game to drive in five runs. Cincinnati stayed in front and went on to win the game, 7-2, and the Series four games to none. The Most Valuable Player was Johnny Bench, who hit .533 and had two homers, a triple and a double, with six runs batted in.

1977

New York Yankees 4, Los Angeles Dodgers 2

In the Western Division of the National League, the Los Angeles Dodgers, under rookie manager Tommy LaSorda, came storming back to take the title, leaving the Cincinnati Reds 10 games behind. In the Eastern Division, the Philadelphia Phillies finished in first place, five games ahead of the Pittsburgh Pirates. But the Dodgers won the playoffs in four games.

This was the year in which the American League expanded yet again by adding the Seattle Mariners (the Seattle Pilots had become the Milwaukee Brewers in 1970) and the Toronto Blue Jays. The Yankees were back as the champions of the Eastern Division of the American League. As late as 7 August, the Yanks were five games out of first place, but they won 13 of the next 14 games and 38 of their last 51, ending up two and a half games ahead of the Baltimore Orioles and the Boston Red Sox. It was the Royals again in the Western Division, beating out the Oakland A's by eight games. Once again, the playoffs went five games. Once again it went down to the ninth inning of the final game, with the Yankees scoring three runs to take the flag.

Manager Billy Martin of the Yankees chose Don Gullett to face Don Sutton in game one of the Series. After a shaky first inning in which the Dodgers scored two runs, the Yankees went on to win, 4-3, in twelve innings. The winner was Sparky Lyle and the loser was Rick Rhoden, both in relief. It was Hunter for the Yanks against Burt Hooten in the second game. But after home runs by third baseman Ron Cey, catcher Steve Yeager and right fielder Reggie Smith had produced five runs for the Dodgers in less than three full innings, the game, for all practical purposes, was over. The contest ended with a 6-1 score.

Tommy John, who had been a 20-game winner for the Dodgers in 1976, started the third game, opposing Mike Torrez. But in the first inning the Yankees jumped on John for three runs — a lead that lasted only to the third inning, when left fielder Dusty Baker hit a three-run homer. Then the Yankees managed to get single runs in the fourth and fifth innings to win the game, 5-3. LaSorda nominated Doug Rau to pitch the fourth game against Ron Guidry. But the Yankees greeted Rau with three runs in the top of the second inning and went on to win, 4-2, on a four-hitter by Guidry.

The Dodgers roared back in the fifth game, getting eight hits and seven runs off Gullett in less than five full innings. Sutton got the 10-4 win. In the sixth game, which turned out to be the final contest, it was Torrez and Hooten on the mound. Dodger first baseman Steve Garvey's triple drove in two runs in the first inning, but Yankee first baseman Chris Chambliss tied the score in the second on a two-run homer. Smith homered in the third, but that was it for the Dodgers. Yankee right fielder Reggie Jackson hit a two-run homer in the fourth and the Yanks went on to win the game, 8-4, and the Series four games to two. Reggie 'Mr October' Jackson, with his five home runs in the Series, was named Most Valuable Player.

LEFT: Dodger third baseman Ron Cey at bat. Cey contributed to Los Angeles' four-homer onslaught in game two as they downed the Yankees, 6-1.

OPPOSITE: The Dodgers' Don Sutton pitched in the Series' first and fifth games. Although LA dropped game one with reliever Rick Rhoden pitching in the twelfth inning, they won game five, 10-4, behind Sutton's strong pitching and their hot batting.

1978

New York Yankees 4, Los Angeles Dodgers 2

In the 1978 season, the same four teams won their divisions as had the year before. Yankee manager Billy Martin, after an altercation with principal owner George Steinbrenner, resigned in July and was replaced by Bob Lemon. When Lemon took over, the Yanks were 10 and a half games behind the Boston Red Sox, but then they began to win. When the Sox lost 14 out of 17 games in September, the two teams ended the season tied for first place. The Yankees won the single tie-breaker game to take the flag in the Eastern Division in the American League. In the Western Division it was the Kansas City Royals for the third consecutive year, and they left the California Angels five games behind. In the playoffs, however, the Yankees beat the Royals three games to one.

Over in the National League the 1978 season seemed in many ways a re-run of the 1977 season. In the Western Division the Los Angeles Dodgers beat out the Cincinnati Reds again, but only after the Reds collapsed on 7 August, losing 15 of their next 21 games while the Dodgers won 22 of their last 37 games. In the Eastern Division, the Philadelphia Phillies and the Pittsburgh Pirates battled it out again, with the Phillies taking their third consecutive division title. In the playoffs the Dodgers took the league championship in three straight games.

So it was the Yankees against the Dodgers in the World Series once again. In the first game, Ed Figueroa took the mound for the Yankees against Tommy John. Going into the top of the seventh, the Dodgers were ahead, 7-0, but the Yankees scored three in the seventh and two in the eighth. Still, they lost to Los Angeles, 11-5. The second game pitted Catfish Hunter of the Yanks against Burt Hooton. The Dodgers took this one, too, 4-3.

Then the Yankees began an unprecedented comeback. Unleashing a 10-hit attack in the third game, they

OPPOSITE TOP: Dodger Davey Lopes is involved in a close play at home as Yankee catcher Thurmon Munson blocks the plate during the '78 World Series. Despite Lopes' three home runs, the Dodgers dropped the Series, four games to two.

LEFT: Reggie Jackson – Mr October – makes his second Series appearance as a New York Yankee. Jackson batted .391 for the Series, with eight RBI's and two round-trippers.

OPPOSITE BOTTOM: The Dodgers' Rick Monday is safe as Yankee second baseman Fred Stanley waits for the throw.

ABOVE: Yankee shortstop
Bucky Dent was named the
Series' MVP after his bat
heated up in games five and
six, when he got three hits in
each contest. Dent batted
.417 with seven RBI's.

LEFT: Dodger southpaw
Tommy John winds up for the
pitch. John won the Series
opener, 11-5.

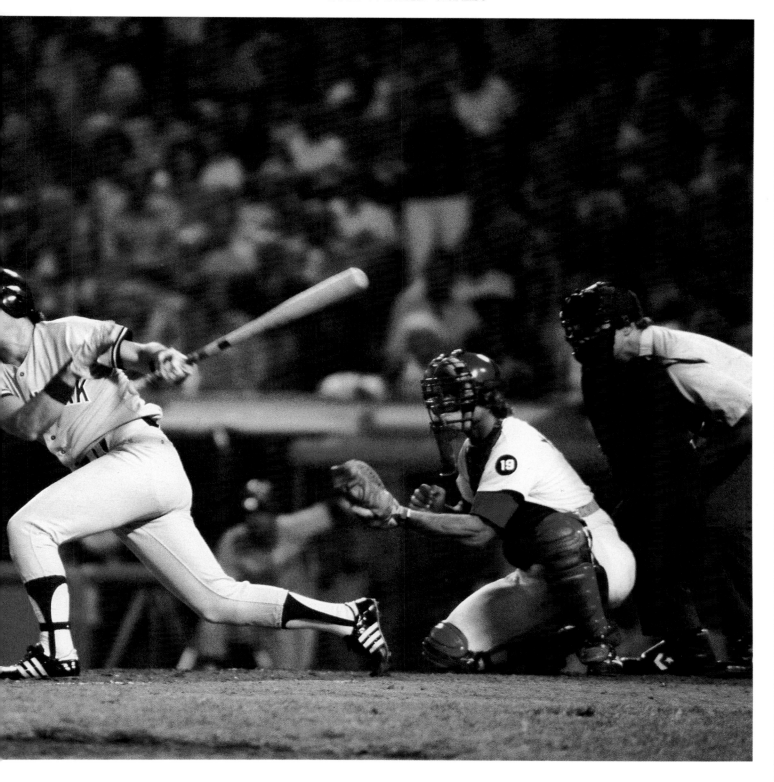

gave Ron Guidry a win over Don Sutton, 5-1. In the fourth game they squeaked by Los Angeles, 4-3, in 10 innings, with Rich 'Goose' Gossage beating Bob Welch, both in relief. It was the Yankees again in the fifth game, this time by a decisive score of 12-2, with Jim Beattie beating Hooton. Los Angeles went out ahead, 1-0 in the first inning of the sixth game on a home run by second baseman Davey Lopes, but that was their only moment of triumph. The Yanks went ahead by scoring three runs in the second and

coasted to a 7-2 win. Hunter had topped Sutton.

So the Yankees were world champions, winning the Series, four games to two, on the strong bats of right fielder Reggie Jackson, left fielder Lou Piniella, shortstop Bucky Dent and catcher Thurman Munson, plus some superb fielding by third baseman Graig Nettles. Thus they became the first team ever to lose the first two games of a World Series and come back to win it in six. Dent, who hit .417, was named the Most Valuable Player.

1979

Pittsburgh Pirates 4, Baltimore Orioles 3

In the National League West the Cincinnati Reds held on in a close race to nose out the Houston Astros by one and a half games. Meanwhile, over in the Eastern Division, it was the Pittsburgh Pirates, on a great team effort, who prevailed. And they went on to beat the Reds in three straight games for the pennant.

The Baltimore Orioles were the class of the American League Eastern Division, winning 102 games and beating out the Milwaukee Brewers by eight games to give manager Earl Weaver his sixth division win in 11 years. It was the California Angels in the West, which was a surprise, since they had been finishing an average of 23 and a half games down in the previous 18 seasons. But the Angels lost to the Orioles in the playoffs, three games to one.

The World Series was a fitting climax to a decade of extremes and upsets. Many of the games were played in the rain and the cold, with the players' fingers sometimes numb. Billed as a 'railroad series' because the cities were so close together, it was a good thing the teams didn't have to fly, because the foul weather might have grounded them.

It was Bruce Kison for the Pirates against Mike Flanagan in the first game. The Orioles jumped off to a 5-0 lead in the first inning, in which the telling blow was a home run by third baseman Doug DeCinces. Baltimore won the game, 5-4. Pittsburgh came back in the second game, winning 3-2 with Don Robinson the winner and Don Stanhouse the loser, both in relief. It was Baltimore's turn in the third game with Scott McGregor going all the way in this 8-4 contest, John Candelaria was the loser.

The Orioles took a commanding three-games-to-one lead in the Series by winning the fourth game, 9-6. The Pirates jumped off to a four-run lead in the second inning and the Orioles came back with three in the third. Going into the eighth it was Pittsburgh, 6-3. But Baltimore lashed back with six runs in that inning, and that was the end of the scoring. Tim Stoddard was the winner and Kent Tekulve the loser.

But the Pirates tightened their belts and took the last three games, 7-1, 4-0 and 4-1, holding Baltimore to just 17 hits and two runs. Bert Blyleven beat Flanagan in the fifth game and Candelaria beat Jim Palmer in the sixth game. In the final game the Orioles struck first with a home run off Jim Bibby, the Pirate starter. But the first baseman Willie 'Pops' Stargell brought the Pirates back. In his first two at bats he had two hits off starter McGregor. When Stargell came up in the sixth inning, he jumped all over the first pitch and slammed a two-run homer, putting the Pirates ahead for good, and they took the championship four games to three. Stargell, with seven extra-base hits, including three home runs, was voted Most Valuable Player.

LEFT: The Pirates' Bert Blyleven on the mound during the '79 Series. Blyleven started game two, which his team won on Don Robinson's relief pitching; then it was Blyleven's turn to gain a victory in relief in game five, when he pitched four shutout innings to beat Baltimore, 7-1.

OPPOSITE TOP: Pirate Phil Garner slides as Oriole Mark Belanger goes for the force-out. Garner went 12 for 24 in the Series.

OPPOSITE BOTTOM: Pirate Willie Stargell gets a standing ovation from the crowd after hammering a two-run homer to put Pittsburgh ahead in game seven.

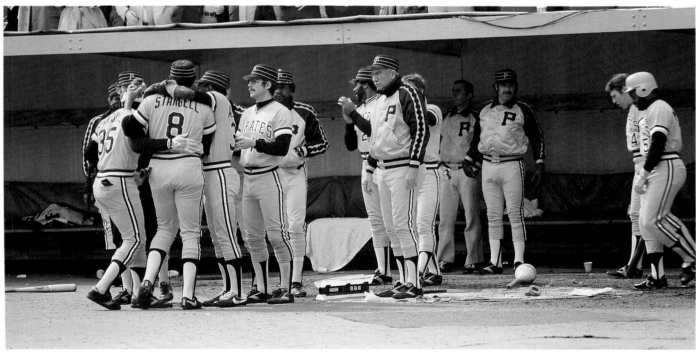

1980

Philadelphia Phillies 4, Kansas City Royals 2

In the American League's Eastern Division it was a race between 1979's winner, the Baltimore Orioles, and 1978's winner, the New York Yankees, but the Yanks prevailed. In the Western Division there was no contest, with the Kansas City Royals leaving the Oakland A's 14 games behind in second place. In the league playoffs, the Royals met the Yankees for the fourth time in five years, and Kansas City beat New York in three straight.

In the National League Western Division, going into the last three games, the Houston Astros had a three-game lead over the Los Angeles Dodgers, and had to face them for the last three games of the season. But the Dodgers took all three to tie for the lead. In the single-game playoff, the Astros came off the ground to win the flag. In the Eastern Division, the talent-laden Philadelphia Phillies couldn't tie up the title until the next-to-last game of the season. The league playoffs were exciting games. They went the full five games, with four of them being extra-inning affairs. But finally the Phillies captured the pennant.

This was only the third time in the Phillies' history that they had made it into a World Series, and in their first, in 1915, they had lost to the Boston Red Sox, four games to one. In 1950 they had been swept away in four straight games by the Yankees. But 1980 proved to be the Phillies' year, when they won four games to two over the Royals. Philadelphia third baseman Mike Schmidt won the Series' Most Valuable Player Award for a .381 batting average, hitting two of the Phillies' three home runs, and a team-leading seven RBI's.

LEFT: The Kansas City Royals' side-arm relief pitcher, Dan Quisenberry, shown in action in the 1980 World Series. Quisenberry pitched in all six games, ending with a win, two losses and one save.

OPPOSITE: The Philadelphia Phillies' Mike Schmidt belts a two-run homer in game five of the Series. With his team-leading seven RBI's, his two homers and his .381 batting average, Schmidt won the Series' MVP Award.

BELOW: The Royals' Clint Hurdle is greeted at home by Willie Wilson as he is about to score. Outfielder Hurdle went 5 for 12 in the Series.

1981

Los Angeles Dodgers 4, New York Yankees 2

This was the year of the strike. The players, fuming over the owners' restricting their rights to negotiate, walked out on 12 June. The strike went on for 50 days, and before it was over 714 games had been cancelled. At the end of the season, it was decided that the four teams leading their divisions when the strike began would face the division leaders from the second half of the season. But there was a flaw in the plan – a team might still have the best record for the season, but still not have led in either half. And that is exactly what happened. In the National League West, the Cincinnati Reds had the best total record, 62 wins and 42 losses, but they came in second in both halves of the season.

It was the Los Angeles Dodgers who won the pre-strike 'pennant' – a half game over the Reds. And the Houston Astros beat out the Reds in the second half of the season, one and a half games ahead of Cincinnati. The Dodgers lost the first two games of the playoffs, but then won the next three for the flag.

The same thing happened in the Eastern Division, with the St Louis Cardinals having the best total record of 59 wins and 43 losses. But the Philadelphia Phillies beat them out by one and a half games in the first half of the season, and the Montreal Expos led them by a half game at the end of the season. In the playoffs, the Expos beat the Phillies, three games to two.

Then came the final playoffs in this endless series. Los Angeles won the first game and Montreal won the next two, but Los Angeles won the final two to become National League champions.

In the American League East, the Yankees came in first in the first half of the season, two games ahead of the Baltimore Orioles, and the Milwaukee Brewers beat out the Boston Red Sox in the second half of the season by one and a half games. New York topped Milwaukee in the playoffs, three games to two.

The Western Division first half ended with the Oakland A's edging out the Texas Rangers by one and a

LEFT: Dodger Davey Lopes gets back to first on an attempted pick-off play in the fifth inning of game six. The Dodgers rallied to beat New York, 9-2, and win the World Series.

ABOVE: Yankee Willie Randolph watches a long ball. With a double, a triple and two home runs, Randolph scored five times on four hits in the Series.

In the final playoffs for the American League championship, New York swept the A's, three games to none.

It was finally time for the World Series. In the first game, New York leaped off to a 3-0 lead in front of the Dodgers in the first inning, then were ahead 5-0 going into the fifth, finally winning 5-3. Ron Guidry was the winner and Jerry Reuss the loser. The Yanks did it again in the second game,

half games. In the second half the Kansas City Royals ended one game up on Oakland. Then the A's swept the playoffs in three games.

OPPOSITE: Dodger third baseman Ron Cey at bat in the 1981 World Series. Cey shared the Series' MVP Award with Pedro Guerrero and Steve Yeager, batting .350 with six RBI's and a home run.

ABOVE: Jubilant Dodger players make their way into the locker room after winning their first World Series under manager Tom Lasorda (in foreground).

RIGHT: Los Angeles ace Fernando Valenzuela pitching during game three.

with Tommy John giving up only three hits in seven innings to shut out Burt Hooten, 3-0.

The Dodgers turned it around in the third game, as their ace pitcher, Fernando Valenzuela, pitched a four-hitter after being staked to three runs in the first inning. Los Angeles went on to win, 5-4. Not to be denied, the Dodgers squeaked out another one-run victory in the fourth game, 8-7. The fifth game was another one-run victory for the Dodgers, when Reuss beat Guidry, 2-1.

Los Angeles completed their comeback in the sixth game, winning 9-2. Although the Yankees scored a run in the third on second baseman Willie Randolph's home run, the Dodgers scored once in the fourth, three times in the fifth and four times in the sixth to put the game out of reach. Hooten had won the game and the Dodgers had won the Series, four games to two. For the first time in history, the Most Valuable Player Award was split three ways – among Dodger third baseman Ron Cey, center fielder Pedro Guerrero and catcher Steve Yeager.

1982

St Louis Cardinals 4, Milwaukee Brewers 3

Two teams did produce an old-fashioned race in the American League East in 1982 – the Milwaukee Brewers and the Baltimore Orioles. As occasionally happens with the chance of scheduling, the two teams found themselves in a four-game series in the final days of the regular season, but the Brewers had a three-game lead and looked like a shoo-in. Then Baltimore won the first three games to tie for the lead. In the final game of the season Don Sutton of the Brewers won decisively, 10-2, and Milwaukee was the division winner. In the Western Division, the California Angels had a struggle with the Kansas City Royals. But the power-packed Angels eventually won the division by three games. In the playoffs, the Angels beat the Brewers in the first two games, then the Brewers turned around and took the next three to become champions of the American League – the first time a team had been down by two games and come back to take the flag.

In the National League West at the end of July, the Atlanta Braves were in first place, nine games ahead of the San Diego Padres and 10 ahead of the Los Angeles Dodgers. But then Atlanta began to lose, and the race came down to the last day of the season. On that day the Dodgers lost to the Giants and the Braves sneaked into first place by one game. The St Louis Cardinals won the Eastern Division by three games over the Philadelphia Phillies, and went on to win the league title by beating the Braves in three straight.

It was all Milwaukee in the first game of the Series, as Mike Caldwell threw a three-hitter at St Louis to shut them out, 10-0, with Bob Forsch the loser. Brewer reliever McClure walked in the winning run in the eighth inning of the second game as the Cardinals won, 5-4. The winner was Bruce Sutter, also in relief. It was St Louis all the way in the third game as they won, 6-2, behind Joaquin Andujar.

Milwaukee tied the Series in the fourth game by scoring six runs in the seventh inning and going on to

LEFT: Cardinal relief pitcher Bruce Sutter is congratulated by his catcher, Darrell Porter, after he held Milwaukee scoreless for two innings for a seventh-game victory.

OPPOSITE BOTTOM LEFT: Milwaukee's pitcher Mike Caldwell gestures triumphantly. Caldwell threw a three-hit shutout in the Series opener, then beat the Cardinals in game five as well.

OPPOSITE TOP: Brewer catcher Ted Simmons readies himself to tag out Cardinal Ozzie Smith.

OPPOSITE BOTTOM RIGHT: The Brewers' Robin Yount hits a long ball. In game five Yount became the first player to have two four-hit Series games.

win, 7-5. Then the Brewers took the Series lead in the fifth game, with Caldwell doing another superb job of pitching by holding the Cardinals to four runs to win, 6-4. St Louis had no problem in the sixth game. They had run up a 13-0 lead going into the ninth inning, the scoring featuring home runs by catcher Darrell Porter and first baseman Keith Hernandez. All that the Brewers could manage was one run in the ninth, and the game ended 13-1.

Andujar won his second game of the Series in the final contest. The game was close until the seventh inning, when the Cardinals scored two runs and went on to win the game, 6-3, and the Series four games to three. Porter, who had done a fine job catching and had collected eight hits in the Series, was voted Most Valuable Player.

1983

Baltimore Orioles 4, Philadelphia Phillies 1

The 1983 season was the year that the drug problem finally couldn't be ignored by organized baseball and its supporters. Some individual players had previously been caught and even sentenced for drug use – particularly cocaine – but in 1983 four players for the Kansas City Royals were found guilty of using cocaine. Many explanations were produced – the high salaries, the nature of life on the road, the general acceptability of drug use in American society – but everyone agreed that professional athletes were going to have to beat this problem.

In the National League, the pennant races produced few surprises. In the Eastern Division, the Philadelphia Phillies had first place all for themselves by 28 September. And there was little surprise in the Western Division, either, where the Los Angeles Dodgers finished the season comfortably in first place. In the playoffs, the Phillies beat the Dodgers three games to two, to win the pennant.

The Baltimore Orioles held off the Detroit Tigers in the American League East. In the Western Division, the Chicago White Sox finally held on to a lead and for the first time since 1959 qualified for post-season play. In the playoffs, the Orioles beat the White Sox in three straight, taking the third game on Tito Landrum's home run.

So once again the Series was billed as a 'railroad Series,' since it pitted the Orioles against their neighbors up the line, the Phillies. The Phillies seemed loaded with talent with the likes of Mike Schmidt, Joe Morgan, Pete Rose and pitcher Steve Carlton, but the Orioles had their own talents such as Eddie Murray and Cal Ripken, Jr. Although the Phillies took the first game, the Orioles went on to sweep the next four and take the Series, four games to one. The Most Valuable Player Award went to Baltimore's catcher Rick Dempsey.

LEFT: The Phillies' Mike Schmidt, who went one for 20 in the Series, takes a big cut. Baltimore catcher Rick Dempsey, crouching behind the plate, won MVP honors with his .385 batting average, including a double and a home run in the fifth and final game.

OPPOSITE: Oriole Scott McGregor lost the Series opener, 2-1, but came back to pitch a five-hit shutout in the Series-clinching game five.

1984

Detroit Tigers 4, San Diego Padres 1

In the Eastern Division of the American League, smart money was behind either the New York Yankees or the Baltimore Orioles. Instead, the Detroit Tigers opened the season with a win, like 12 other major-league teams. But unlike the other 12, Detroit just went on winning and winning, setting a record by winning 35 out of their first 40 games. At one point they also won 17 straight games on the road, and by 18 September the Tigers had clinched first place in the division, and their manager, Sparky Anderson, would end up the season as the first manager to lead two different clubs with 100-plus victories. In the Western Division, the Kansas City Royals ended up three games in front of the California Angels. The Tigers took the playoffs in three games straight.

As the season drew to a close in the Eastern Division of the National League, pennant fever swept Chicago Cubs' fans. The Cubs won the division, clinching it by 24 September – the first championship of any kind they had won since 1945. In the West it was the San Diego Padres. In the playoffs the Cubs wiped the Padres out in the first game, 13-0, hitting five home runs in the game – a playoff record. And then Chicago won the second, 4-2. But then the series moved to San Diego and the Padres won the last three games to win the National League pennant.

The first game of the World Series was a squeaker, with both teams garnering eight hits. The Tigers scored one run in the first, and the Padres countered with two in the same inning. But Detroit went ahead to stay, with two in the fifth to win the game, 3-2. Jack Morris was the winner and Mark Thurmond the loser. In the second game, the Tigers wasted no time demonstrating their superiority by getting three runs in the top of the first inning. But that was all they could get, as San Diego scored one in the first, one in the fourth

LEFT: During the 1984 National League Championship Series, San Diego's first baseman Steve Garvey sets himself for the tag in a pick-off attempt. 1984 was the Cubs' and the Padres' first playoff appearance.

OPPOSITE: The Tigers' Alan Trammell fouls one off. The Series MVP would belt two two-run homers in game four, a 4-2 decision.

and three in the fifth to win the game, 5-3.

The Tigers once again leaped out to a lead in the third game, scoring four runs in the second inning, two on a home run by Castillo and one on a walk. This time they held on to the lead and won the game, 5-2. Milt Wilcox was the winner and Tim Lollar was the loser. In the fourth game, Detroit took a commanding three-games-to-one lead by winning the game, 4-2, once again jumping out in front early on two runs in the first inning. Morris won his second game and Eric Show was the loser.

The fifth game turned out to be the final contest. Once again the Tigers got in front early, scoring three runs in the first inning. The Padres tied it up in the fourth, but the Tigers prevailed, 8-2, with Aurelio Lopez the winner and Hawkins the loser, and took the Series four games to one. Detroit shortstop Alan Trammell, who collected an astonishing nine hits in five games, was named the Series' MVP. The only thing that marred Detroit's spectacular season was the riotous celebration in Detroit after their Series clincher, which left one bystander dead.

1985

Kansas City Royals 4, St Louis Cardinals 3

By the midseason All-Star break, the St Louis Cardinals were in first place in the Eastern Division of the National League, while in the Western Division, the Los Angeles Dodgers were in first place by a half game. When the season ended, the Cards had won by three games over the New York Mets and the Dodgers were the winners by five and a half games over the Cincinnati Reds. The Cardinals swept the playoffs, 12-2, 3-2 and 7-5.

The experts picked the Toronto Blue Jays to win the Eastern Division in the American League. The Jays got off to a great start and by mid-season were in first place, two and a half games in front of the New York Yankees. New York was unable to catch Toronto, ending up two games out. Over in the Western Division, the Kansas City Royals were also picked to win, but by mid-season, they were seven and a half games out of first place. They did, however, manage to win the division, but only by one game ahead of the California Angels. The Royals beat the Jays in the playoffs, but it took seven games, with Toronto winning the first two and the fourth game.

In the first game of the Series, St Louis came from behind to capture the contest, 3-1. After the Royals scored one run in the first inning, the Cards scored one run in the third, the fourth and the ninth. The winner was John Tudor and the loser was Danny Jackson. The Cards did it again in the second game, winning 4-2, but it was a thriller. The Royals tallied two runs in the fourth, and the prospects for the Cards looked bleak going into the ninth inning. But they scored one run, and then Gary Pendleton hit a bases-loaded double to provide the winning three runs. Ken Dayley was the winner and Charlie Leibrandt was the loser.

Kansas City snapped back in the third game, with Bret Saberhagen facing Joaquin Andujar. Saberhagen scattered six hits to win, 6-1, with two Royal runs in the fourth, fifth and eighth innings. St Louis won the

OPPOSITE TOP: The Royals' George Brett watches a line drive. Despite the Cardinals' efforts to pitch around Brett, he held the Series' highest batting average for a starting player, hitting .370.

OPPOSITE BOTTOM: The Cardinals' ace, John Tudor, follows through on a pitch in the Series' seventh game. Tudor, who had allowed one run in 15 and two-thirds innings, did not last past the third inning in game seven as the Royals romped to an 11-0 victory.

LEFT: Kansas City's Bret Saberhagen gets ready to uncork one in game seven, a complete game shutout victory. The righthander's two Series victories, achieved with an 0.50 ERA for 18 innings, would earn him the MVP Award.

fourth game, with Tudor shutting out Kansas City, 3-0, and Gregg Landrum hitting the eventual game-winning home run in the second. Bud Black was the loser.

The Royals had to win the fifth game, and win it they did, 6-1, behind the five-hit pitching of Jackson, who beat Bob Forsch. And Kansas City did it again in the sixth game, 2-1, to tie the Series. It was a real cliffhanger. The first run was scored by the Cardinals in the eighth inning. But in the bottom of the ninth, the Royals scored the two winning runs to tie up the Series. The winner was Dan Quisenberry and the loser, Todd Worrell – both in relief.

So it all came down to the seventh, final game. And it was no contest, the Royals winning 11-0, going ahead for good with two runs in the second inning. The winner was Saberhagen again and the loser was Tudor. Kansas City took the Series four games to three, and Saberhagen, with his two wins, was voted the Series' Most Valuable Player.

1986

New York Mets 4, Boston Red Sox 3

It was the consensus of sportswriters and oddsmakers that the New York Mets would go all the way in the Eastern Division of the National League in 1986. And indeed they did, moving into the lead on 23 April and never being headed, ending up an astonishing 21 and a half games ahead of the second-place Philadelphia Phillies. In the Western Division the Houston Astros fought off the San Francisco Giants and the Cincinnati Reds, finishing 10 games ahead of the pack. The Mets won the playoffs four games to two, piling up 22 runs to the Astros' 17.

In the Eastern Division of the American League, the spotlight descended on the Boston Red Sox on 29 April when Roger Clemens astonished baseball fans by setting a new modern major-league record of 20 strikeouts in a nine-inning game. He went on to win his first 14 games, and the Sox took over first place on 15 May. Boston finished in first place, five and a half games ahead of the New York Yankees. In the West it was the California Angels, five games ahead of the Texas Rangers. The Angels took the first game of the playoffs, 8-1, collapsed in the second, losing 9-2, and won the third, 5-3. In the fourth game, the Sox took a 3-0 lead in the ninth, blew it, and then lost, 4-3, in the eleventh. In the deciding fifth game the Angels held a 5-2 lead going into the ninth inning, but the Red Sox scored four runs in the top of the inning. The Angels tied it up in the bottom of the inning, but Boston went on to take the game in the eleventh inning, 7-6. Then the Sox won the sixth and seventh games, 10-4 and 8-1.

In the Series, Boston won the first game, Bruce Hurst beating Ron Darling, 1-0, with Boston getting but five hits and New York four. The Red Sox won the second game, too, when they racked up 18 hits to triumph, 9-3, with Steve Crawford beating Dwight Gooden. In the third game the Mets finally woke up, winning 7-1, with Bob Ojeda beating Oil Can Boyd.

LEFT: The Mets' ace, Dwight Gooden, gets ready to unleash some heat. Dr K did not have the antidote as he faltered in both of his World Series starts.

OPPOSITE: New York's Daryl Strawberry makes contact. The Strawman hit a decisive home run in game seven off Red Sox pitcher Al Nipper to lead his team to a World Series title.

New York tied the Series in the fourth game by winning 6-2, as Ron Darling beat Al Nipper. Then the Sox went ahead, three games to two, with a fifth-game victory. The Red Sox needed but one victory to win their first World Series since 1918. Pitching for Boston in game six was Clemens, and for the Mets was Ojeda. The Red Sox staked Clemens to a two-run lead, but by the seventh inning Clemens had developed a blister on his hand, so manager John McNamara went to his bullpen and brought in Calvin Schiraldi. With a man on first, Schiraldi threw away a bunt, and the Mets had men on first and second. They got a man to third, and catcher Gary Carter hit a sacrifice fly to tie the score at 2-2. In the tenth inning, the Red Sox gained a lead when center fielder Dave Henderson hit a home run, and this was followed by two more hits to make the score 4-2. But the Mets came back in the bottom

of the tenth. With two out, catcher Gary Carter and pinch-hitter Kevin Mitchell singled. Third baseman Ray Knight singled, scoring Carter. Mitchell scored on a wild pitch to tie it up, and Knight scored the winning run on an error by Sox first baseman Bill Buckner. The Mets won, 5-4, with Rick Aguilera the winner and Schiraldi the loser, both in relief.

So it came down to the seventh game, and for a while it looked as though Boston might pull it off,

after taking a 3-0 lead in the second inning. But the Mets tied it up in the sixth. In came Schiraldi again to face Knight, and he gave up a home run to put New York ahead. The Mets tallied two more runs in the inning. The Sox came back in the eighth with two runs, but the Mets matched that in the bottom of the inning and won the game, 8-5, and the Series, four games to three. Knight, with his nine hits and seven runs batted in, was voted the MVP.

1987

Minnesota Twins 4, St Louis Cardinals 3

In many ways, the story of the final standings in both leagues in 1987 was not so much that the winners won, but rather that the losers collapsed. In the Western Division of the National League, the Cincinnati Reds were in first place from 29 May to 19 August. On 5 July, they were even 11 games in first place with a 46-35 record. Then the bottom dropped out and by 1 September they were in third place with a 64-68 record. The Giants held on, ending six games ahead of the Reds.

In the National League East, the St Louis Cardinals pretty much held on all the way, but it was touch and go, with the New York Mets and the Montreal Expos giving them fits. Both clubs were in the race down to the final week, mostly because of the terrible string of injuries suffered by the Redbirds. Star pitcher John Tudor was out for many weeks with a broken leg, and slugger Jack Clark was out for part of the regular season, the playoffs and the World Series. (Things were so bad that the Cardinals, when they made it to the Series, voted their orthopedist a half-share of the Series' money.) At any rate, St Louis won the East, ending three games ahead of the Mets and four in front of the Expos.

The collapsers in the American League East were the Toronto Blue Jays. It had been a battle between the Jays and the Detroit Tigers until the final week of the season. With seven games to play, Toronto was three and a half games ahead of the Tigers. Then, plagued with injuries, they proceeded to drop all seven games (the Tigers beating them in the last three) and Detroit won the title by two games.

The California Angels were only a half game out of first place in the American League West on 5 August. They went on to lose 29 games and win but 15. Still, at the end of August, they were only three games back, but they proceeded to lose 15 out of 20, and the Minnesota Twins, with their puny .525 winning percentage, won the title by two games over Kansas City.

OPPOSITE: The umpire gets ready to make the call as the San Francisco baserunner slides into home during the 1987 National League Championship Series between the Giants and the Cardinals.

ABOVE: Rookie Tiger catcher Matt Nokes hitting off his front foot in the 1987 American League Championship Series between the Tigers and the Twins.

In the National League playoffs, the Cardinals jumped off to a lead with a 5-3 win in the first game behind Greg Mathews, who beat the Giants' Rick Reuschel. The Giants tied the series with a 5-0 win in the second game, Dave Dravecky beating John Tudor. The Cards came back in the third game, winning a squeaker, 6-5, and then San Francisco tied the series, 4-2, and took the lead in the next game, 6-3. All the Giants needed was one more win, but the Redbirds came back to shut out San Francisco in the final two games, 1-0 and 6-0, to take the National League pennant.

The Twins had an easier time with the Tigers. They won the first game, 8-5, scoring four times in the eighth inning. They did it again, 6-3, in the second game. Finally, the Tigers won their first game, 7-6. But Minnesota nailed down the coffin with two straight wins, 5-3 and 9-5.

In the Series' opener in the noisy Metrodome, it was Frank Viola of the Twins opposing Joe Magrane of the Cards. Viola had been scheduled to be the best man at his brother's wedding that day, but passed it up to open the Series and give up only five hits in eight innings in the Twins' 10-1 blowout of the Cardinals. All Minnesota needed was their seven runs in the fateful fourth inning in this first World Series game played indoors.

The fourth inning was another disaster for the Cardinals in the second game, which the Twins won, 8-4, with their six-run fourth. This time the

winner was Bert Blyleven and the loser was Danny Cox.

Then the Series switched to St Louis, and it was the Cardinals' turn. Tudor was the starter again, and this time he survived the fourth inning. But the Twins scored once in the sixth, and Les Straker, the oldest rookie to start a Series game in 20 years, was in good shape, having given up but four hits. Then Juan Berenguer came in in the seventh and gave up four hits and three runs in a third of an inning. St Louis won, 3-1, with Tudor the winner and Berenguer the loser.

Feeling at home in Busch Stadium, the Cards won the fourth game, 7-2, to tie the Series. This time it was their turn to score big in the fourth inning, where they tallied six times. The hero of the game was Tom Lawless, who was playing third base because Terry Pendleton had strained ribs. Lawless, who had played only three games during the season, collecting only two hits, hit a three-run homer in the fourth. It was only the second round-tripper of his career. Viola was the loser, and Bob Forsch, in relief, was the winner.

The Redbirds made it three in a row in the fifth game, winning 4-2. Danny Cox was the winner and Blyleven was the loser, and the game was won by the Cards' daring base running. They stole six.

Then it was back to Minneapolis for the sixth game, and Manager Tom Kelly of the Twins opted to start Straker, while Whitey Herzog chose Tudor again. For a while, it was a nail-biter. St Louis scored one in the top of the first, and Minnesota countered with two in that same inning. The Cards tied it with another run in the second and jumped ahead with two in the fourth and one in the top of the fifth. Then the roof caved in on the Redbirds as the Twins tallied four in the fifth, four in the sixth and one in the eighth to slaughter St Louis, 11-5. Dan Schatzeder, in relief, was the winner, and Tudor was the loser.

So it came down to the final game in the Minneapolis Metrodome in which Joe Magrane and Frank Viola were the starting pitchers. In the second inning, St Louis scored two and Minnesota scored one, but the never-say-die Twins tied the score in the fifth. And that was all for the Cards. The Twins scored once more in the sixth and once in the eighth to win, 4-2. The fans went wild – shouting, singing and waving 'homer hankies.' Viola won his second game of the Series and Cox, in relief, was the loser.

Not only was this the first World Series championship for the Twins, but also it was the first Series to go the limit and have the home team win every game – and it was the first world championship for rookie manager Tom Kelly. Viola was voted the Most Valuable Player in the Fall Classic.

OPPOSITE: Cardinal Jose Oquendo, who played first base for the injured Jack Clark in the 1987 Series, slides into home where Twin catcher Tim Laudner waits with the ball.

ABOVE: Jubilant Twins celebrate their first World Series championship ever, after winning game seven in the Metrodome.

RIGHT: Minnesota's lefthander Frank Viola unwinds. Viola pitched superbly in three Series games, winning game one, losing game four on Tom Lawless' three-run homer, but coming back to earn the decisive seventh-game victory, and the Series' MVP Award.

World Series Most Valuable Players

1955 Johnny Podres
pitcher, Brooklyn Dodgers

1958 Bob Turley
pitcher, New York Yankees

1960 Bobby Richardson
second baseman, New York Yankees

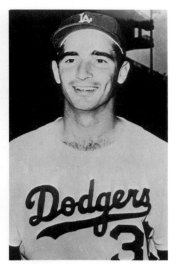

1963/65 Sandy Koufax
pitcher, Los Angeles Dodgers

1956 Don Larsen
pitcher, New York Yankees

1959 Larry Sherry
pitcher, Los Angeles Dodgers

1961 Whitey Ford
pitcher, New York Yankees

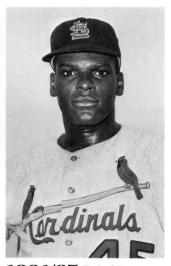

1964/67 Bob Gibson
pitcher, St Louis Cardinals

1957 Lew Burdette (left) pitcher, Milwaukee Braves

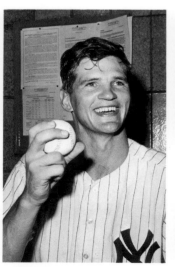

1962 Ralph Terry
pitcher, New York Yankees

1966 Frank Robinson
right fielder, Baltimore Orioles

1968 Mickey Lolich
pitcher, Detroit Tigers

1971 Roberto Clemente
right fielder, Pittsburgh Pirates

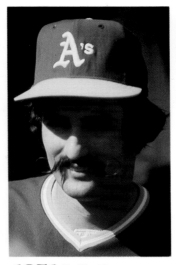

1974 Rollie Fingers
pitcher, Oakland A's

1978 Bucky Dent
shortstop, New York Yankees

1969 Donn Clendenon
first baseman, New York Mets

1972 Gene Tenace
catcher, Oakland A's

1975 Pete Rose
third baseman, Cincinnati Reds

1979 Willie Stargell
first baseman, Pittsburgh
Pirates

1970 Brooks Robinson
third baseman, Baltimore
Orioles

1973 Reggie Jackson
center fielder-right fielder,
Oakland A's
1977 right fielder, New York
Yankees

1976 Johnny Bench
catcher, Cincinnati Reds

1980 Mike Schmidt third
baseman, Philadelphia Phillies

1981 Ron Cey third baseman, LA Dodgers

1981 Pedro Guerrero center fielder, LA Dodgers

1981 Steve Yeager catcher, LA Dodgers

1982 Darrell Porter catcher, St Louis Cardinals

1984 Alan Trammell shortstop, Detroit Tigers

1986 Ray Knight third baseman, New York Mets

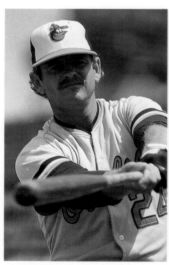

1983 Rick Dempsey catcher, Baltimore Orioles

1985 Bret Saberhagen pitcher, Kansas City Royals

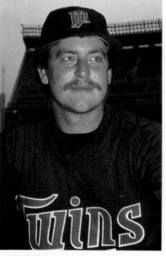

1987 Frank Viola pitcher, Minnesota Twins

LIFETIME PITCHING LEADERS

WINS
1. Whitey Ford 10
2. Bob Gibson 7
2. Red Ruffing 7
2. Allie Reynolds 7
5. Lefty Gomez 6
5. Chief Bender 6
5. Waite Hoyt 6
8. Jack Coombs 5
8. Three Finger Brown 5
8. Herb Pennock 5
8. Christy Mathewson 5
8. Vic Raschi 5
8. Catfish Hunter 5

WINNING PERCENTAGE
1. Lefty Gomez 1.000
1. Jack Coombs 1.000
1. Herb Pennock 1.000
1. Monte Pearson 1.000
1. Babe Adams 1.000
1. Mickey Lolich 1.000
1. George Pipgras 1.000
1. Babe Ruth 1.000
1. Tom Zachary 1.000
1. Jerry Koosman 1.000
1. Jesse Barnes 1.000
1. Ed Raulbach 1.000
1. Luis Tiant 1.000
1. Jack Billingham 1.000

EARNED RUN AVERAGE
1. Jack Billingham .... .36
2. Harry Brecheen .... .83
3. Babe Ruth .... .87
4. Sherry Smith .... .89
5. Sandy Koufax .... .95
6. Hippo Vaughn 1.00
7. Monte Pearson 1.01
8. Christy Mathewson 115
9. Babe Adams 1.29
10. Eddie Plank 1.32
11. Rollie Fingers 1.35
12. Bill Hallahan 1.36

GAMES
1. Whitey Ford 22
2. Rollie Fingers 16
3. Allie Reynolds 15
3. Bob Turley 15
5. Clay Carroll 14
6. Clem Labine 13
7. Waite Hoyt 12
7. Catfish Hunter 12
7. Art Nehf 12
10. Paul Derringer 11
10. Carl Erskine 11
10. Rube Marquard 11
10. Christy Mathewson 11
10. Vic Raschi 11

BASES ON BALLS
1. Whitey Ford 34
2. Allie Reynolds 32
2. Art Nehf 32
4. Jim Palmer 31
5. Bob Turley 29
6. Paul Derringer 27
6. Red Ruffing 27
8. Don Gullet 26
8. Burleigh Grimes 26
10. Vic Raschi 25
11. Carl Erskine 24
12. Bill Hallahan 23
13. Waite Hoyte 22
14. Jack Coombs 21
14. Chief Bender 21

COMPLETE GAMES
1. Christy Mathewson 10
2. Chief Bender 9
3. Bob Gibson 8
4. Red Ruffing 7
4. Whitey Ford 7
6. George Mullin 6
6. Eddie Plank 6
6. Art Nehf 6
6. Waite Hoyt 6

INNINGS PITCHED
1. Whitey Ford 146
2. Christy Mathewson 102
3. Red Ruffing 86
4. Chief Bender 85
5. Waite Hoyt 84
6. Bob Gibson 81
7. Art Nehf 79
8. Allie Reynolds 77
9. Jim Palmer 65
10. Catfish Hunter 63
11. George Earnshaw 63
12. Joe Bush 61
13. Vic Raschi 60
14. Rube Marquard 59
15. George Mullin 58

SAVES
1. Rollie Fingers 6
2. Allie Reynolds 4
2. Johnny Murphy 4
4. Roy Face 3
4. Herb Pennock 3
4. Kent Tekulve 3
4. Firpo Marbery 3
4. Will McEnaney 3
4. Tug McGraw 3

STRIKEOUTS
1. Whitey Ford 94
2. Bob Gibson 92
3. Allie Reynolds 62
4. Sandy Koufax 61
4. Red Ruffing 61
6. Chief Bender 59
7. George Earnshaw 56
8. Waite Hoyt 49
9. Christy Mathewson 48
10. Bob Turley 46
11. Jim Palmer 44
12. Vic Raschi 43

SHUTOUTS
1. Christy Mathewson 4
2. Three Finger Brown 3
2. Whitey Ford 3
4. Bill Hallahan 2
4. Lew Burdette 2
4. Bill Dinneen 2
4. Sandy Koufax 2
4. Allie Reynolds 2
4. Art Nehf 2
4. Bob Gibson 2

LOSSES
1. Whitey Ford 8
2. Eddie Plank 5
2. Schoolboy Rowe 5
2. Joe Bush 5
2. Rube Marquard 5
2. Christy Mathewson 5

LIFETIME BATTING LEADERS

BATTING AVERAGE
1. Pepper Martin 418
2. Lou Brock 391
3. George Brett 373
3. Thurman Munson 373
4. Hank Aaron 364
5. Frank Baker 363
6. Roberto Clemente 362
7. Lou Gehrig 361
8. Reggie Jackson 357
9. Carl Yastrzemski 352
10. Earle Combs 350
11. Stan Hack 348
12. Joe Jackson 345
13. Jimmie Foxx 344
14. Julian Javier 333
14. Billy Martin 333

GAMES
1. Yogi Berra 75
2. Mickey Mantle 65
3. Elston Howard 54
4. Hank Bauer 53
4. Gil McDougald 53
6. Phil Rizzuto 52
7. Joe DiMaggio 51
8. Frankie Frisch 50
9. Pee Wee Reese 44
10. Roger Maris 41
10. Babe Ruth 41
12. Carl Furillo 40
13. Jim Gilliam 39
13. Gil Hodges 39
13. Bill Skowron 39

AT BATS
1. Yogi Berra 259
2. Mickey Mantle 230
3. Joe DiMaggio 199
4. Frankie Frisch 197
5. Gil McDougald 190
6. Hank Bauer 188
7. Phil Rizzuto 183
8. Elston Howard 171
9. Pee Wee Reese 169
10. Roger Maris 152
11. Jim Gilliam 147
12. Tony Kubek 146
13. Bill Dickey 145
14. Jackie Robinson 137
15. Duke Snider 133
15. Bill Skowron 133

TOTAL BASES
1. Mickey Mantle 123
2. Yogi Berra 117
3. Babe Ruth 96
4. Lou Gehrig 87
5. Joe DiMaggio 84
6. Duke Snider 79
7. Hank Bauer 75
8. Reggie Jackson 74
8. Frankie Frisch 74
10. Gil McDougald 72
11. Bill Skowron 69
12. Elston Howard 66
13. Goose Goslin 63

STOLEN BASES
1. Lou Brock 14
1. Eddie Collins 14
3. Frank Chance 10
3. Davey Lopes 10
3. Phil Rizzuto 10
6. Honus Wagner 9
6. Frankie Frisch 9
8. Johnny Evers 8
9. Pepper Martin 7
9. Joe Morgan 7
11. Jimmy Slagle 6
11. Bobby Tolan 6
11. Joe Tinker 6
11. Maury Wills 6
11. Jackie Robinson 6

HITS
1. Yogi Berra 71
2. Mickey Mantle 59
3. Frankie Frisch 58
4. Joe DiMaggio 54
5. Pee Wee Reese 46
5. Hank Bauer 46
7. Phil Rizzuto 45
7. Gil McDougald 45
9. Lou Gehrig 43
10. Eddie Collins 42
10. Babe Ruth 42
10. Elston Howard 42
13. Bobby Richardson 40

DOUBLES
1. Frankie Frisch 10
1. Yogi Berra 10
3. Pete Fox 9
3. Jack Barry 9
3. Carl Furillo 9
6. Lou Gehrig 8
6. Duke Snider 8

TRIPLES
1. Tommy Leach 4
1. Billy Johnson 4
1. Tris Speaker 4
4. Buck Freeman 3
4. Freddy Parent 3
4. Chick Stahl 3
4. Bobby Brown 3
4. Dave Concepcion 3
4. Tim McCarver 3
4. Billy Martin 3
4. Lou Gehrig 3
4. Bob Meusal 3
4. Hank Bauer 3
4. Frankie Frisch 3

HOME RUNS
1. Mickey Mantle 18
2. Babe Ruth 15
3. Yogi Berra 12
4. Duke Snider 11
5. Reggie Jackson 10
5. Lou Gehrig 10
7. Frank Robinson 8
7. Bill Skowron 8
7. Joe DiMaggio 8
10. Goose Goslin 7
10. Hank Bauer 7
10. Gil McDougald 7

RUNS BATTED IN
1. Mickey Mantle 40
2. Yogi Berra 39
3. Lou Gehrig 35
4. Babe Ruth 33
5. Joe DiMaggion 30
6. Bill Skowron 29
7. Duke Snider 26
8. Reggie Jackson 24
8. Bill Dickey 24
8. Hank Bauer 24
8. Gil McDougald 24
12. Hank Greenberg 22
13. Gil Hodges 21

RUNS
1. Mickey Mantle 42
2. Yogi Berra 41
3. Babe Ruth 37
4. Lou Gehrig 30
5. Joe DiMaggio 27
6. Roger Maris 26
7. Elston Howard 25
8. Gil McDougald 23
9. Jackie Robinson 22
10. Gene Woodling 21
10. Reggie Jackson 21
10. Duke Snider 21
10. Phil Rizzuto 21
10. Hank Bauer 21

189

Acknowledgments

The author and publisher would like to thank the following people for their help: Design 23 for the design, Barbara Paulding Thrasher for the editing, Donna Cornell Muntz for the picture research, Robert Muntz and Jeff Thrasher for technical assistance, and Cynthia Kelin for the index. Special thanks to Pat Kelly, Photo Collection Manager, and staff at The National Baseball Hall of Fame and Museum, Inc; and to Katherine G Bang and staff at UPI/Bettmann Newsphotos.

Picture Credits